HOCKEY GOALTENDING

BRIAN DACCORD

HUMAN KINETICS

Library of Congress Cataloging-in-Publication Data

Daccord, Brian,   1964-
    Hockey goaltending / Brian Daccord.
        p.   cm.
    Includes index.
    ISBN 0-88011-791-5
    1. Hockey--Goalkeeping.   2. Hockey goalkeepers--Training of.
    3. Roller hockey.   I. Title.
    GV848.76.D33   1998   98-12412
    796.962'27--DC21   CIP

ISBN: 0-88011-791-5

Acquisitions Editor: Martin Barnard; **Developmental Editor:** Elaine Mustain; **Assistant Editors:** Melinda Graham, Phil Natividad; **Copyeditor:** Brian Mustain; **Proofreader:** Jim Burns; **Indexer:** Craig Brown; **Graphic Designer:** Robert Reuther; **Graphic Artist:** Yvonne Winsor; **Photo Editor:** Boyd LaFoon; **Cover Designer:** Jack Davis; **Photographer (cover):** © NHL Images; **Photographer (interior):** iv, 21, 173 © Davis Barber; v, 1, 51, 111 © Picture Desk/Robert Skeoch; 73, 129 © Tim De Frisco; 155 © Jim McIsaac/Bruce Bennett Studios. All others by Tom Roberts/Human Kinetics, unless otherwise credited; **Illustrator:** Joe Bellis; **Printer:** United Graphics

Human Kinetics books are available at special discounts for bulk purchase. Special editions or book excerpts can also be created to specification. For details, contact the Special Sales Manager at Human Kinetics.

Printed in the United States of America   10   9   8   7   6   5   4   3   2   1

Human Kinetics
Web site: http://www.humankinetics.com/

United States: Human Kinetics
P.O. Box 5076
Champaign, IL 61825-5076
1-800-747-4457
e-mail: humank@hkusa.com

Canada: Human Kinetics
475 Devonshire Road Unit 100
Windsor, ON N8Y 2L5
1-800-465-7301 (in Canada only)
e-mail: humank@hkcanada.com

Europe: Human Kinetics
P.O. Box IW14
Leeds LS16 6TR, United Kingdom
(44) 1132 781708
e-mail: humank@hkeurope.com

Australia: Human Kinetics
57A Price Avenue
Lower Mitcham, South Australia 5062
(088) 277 1555
e-mail: humank@hkaustralia.com

New Zealand: Human Kinetics
P.O. Box 105-231, Auckland 1
(09) 523 3462
e-mail: humank@hknewz.com

*To my wife Daniela and my son Joël—the thrill of
having them in my life is far greater than anything I've
accomplished on or off the ice.*

Acknowledgments

Thanks to all the hockey people who have encouraged and taught me through the years, and to my parents. Without their support and dedication, I could never have reached my goals. I would also like to thank the following.

Huron Hockey: Paul O'Dacre, Bill Fehrman, Brent Brekke, and Tom Fogu

Chicago Freeze Hockey Club: Marc Carlson and Chris Newman

Miller Goaltending Equipment: Bret Hayward

I-Tech Sports Products, Inc.: Robin Burns

Fox Valley Ice Arena & Fitness Club

Fox Valley Ice Arena Pro Shop: Jeff Dupuis

The Dome in Elgin, IL: Tony Barico

The Valley Jr. Warriors: Paul Gilmartin and John Gilmartin

The All-American Goalie School: Mike Geragosian

Jim Webster, who helped bring this project to fruition

Human Kinetics: Martin Barnard, Elaine Mustain, Tom Roberts, Phil Natividad, Bob Reuther, and Yvonne Winsor

Daniela Daccord for all her hard work on this book

Mike Duffy, Lisa Keohane, Bruno Knutti, and Michael Roggo

Contents

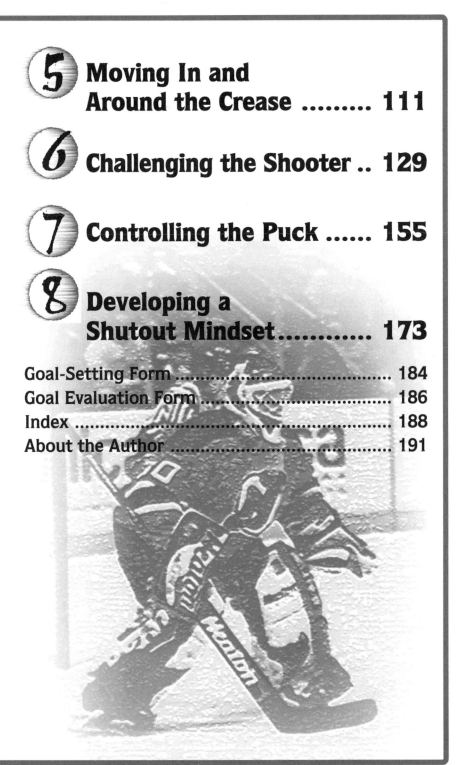

Foreword

My main goal when I started to play hockey was to one day hold the Stanley Cup aloft. In 1995, I realized my dream when the New Jersey Devils captured hockey's Holy Grail. The goaltender's position is arguably the most important in team sports, but only recently has it received the commitment to specialized coaching and skills development that it deserves. In the NHL, I've been blessed with an outstanding mentor in Jacques Caron.

Growing up in Montreal, I read the one book I could find on goaltending about 20 times and always wished there was more information available about becoming a better netminder. It's gratifying to finally find a comprehensive book, Brian Daccord's *Hockey Goaltending*, that covers all facets of our demanding position, including equipment, conditioning and off-ice training, technical skills, and mental approach. Daccord's knowledge, thoroughness, attention to detail, and enthusiasm for the position make it clear that he is a member of the "Fraternity of Goaltenders" who is uniquely qualified to be a "mentor-in-print" for players. Youth coaches will also gain valuable insight (along with useful drills) to help them understand and coach the position effectively.

Since I've been in the NHL I've learned lots of little things that I wish I'd known much earlier. For example, if you follow the puck with your stick, you'll always be in good position. *Hockey Goaltending* delivers countless tips such as this. Knowing how to do these little things right adds up to some big saves in game situations.

"Don't try to be like anybody else, try to be like everybody," is important advice my goalie coach gave me. If you see Patrick Roy or Dominik Hasek do something that you think might work for you, try to incorporate it into your game. *Hockey Goaltending* shows you how to use different techniques and approaches to mold your individual style and give you the goaltending versatility you need.

There are many ingredients that go into the makeup of a great goaltender. Natural athletic ability, a relentless work ethic, and a disciplined lifestyle are certainly important factors. But it's also great to have a step-by-step manual that serves as a job description for the tasks you want to accomplish. Brian Daccord has fired a winner with *Hockey Goaltending*, and there will be fewer game-winning goals scored on its readers because of it!

Introduction

We are in a transition period for goaltenders. Like the game itself, the position of goaltender and the fundamentals considered necessary for success are evolving. In the past, success in goaltending was based on reflexes and quickness, whereas recently greater emphasis has been placed on positioning and taking away zones of the net. *Hockey Goaltending* will help you take your level of play to new heights by showing you how to combine athleticism, desire, and understanding how to cut down the shooter's possibilities to score. Whether you are an ice hockey or an in-line hockey goaltender, male or female, this book will show you how to keep the puck out of the net!

Initial reaction to a shooting situation is to take away the greatest opportunity a puck has to get by you. With longer shots, this is done by projecting forward on your angle. In many instances—such as a rebound, a cross-ice pass, or an attacker in tight—your smartest approach is covering the majority of the net and thereby limiting the shooter's chances to score. Martin Brodeur demonstrates game in and game out how positioning and playing percentages can cut down a shooter's odds of scoring, which in turn cuts down Brodeur's "goals against" average. You can do the same by studying and practicing the techniques and tactics presented in the pages that follow.

Because of the speed of the game and the increased size of the players nowadays, goaltenders need the ability to cover as much of the net as possible. A great example of a progressive strategy for doing this is the calculated shaft-down technique, perfected by Eddie Belfour, which requires shooters to pinpoint a small area of the net strategically left exposed and virtually eliminates the possibility of a soft goal along the ice. This means being square to the puck, extending the stick and gloves forward, cutting down the trajectory (or "angle of flight") the shot must take to beat you, and putting yourself in position to block its path rather than simply relying on reflexes. *Hockey Goaltending* will teach you this and other cutting-edge techniques, and it will also show you how to sharpen your basic skills.

Mike Richter, who almost single-handedly won the World Cup in 1996 for Team USA, is an example of a goaltender who utilizes progressive strategies in combination with sound goaltending basics. Richter uses his experience to know when to try to cover as much of the net as possible, or when to play the shot "straight up" by relying on reflexes and experience on reading where the puck is headed. His ability to apply the best strategy at the right times makes him one of the most dominant goaltenders in the NHL today.

Coaches must respect that there are different schools of thought on how a goaltender should play certain situations. Make sure you have an open line of communication with your players. Remember that no matter how knowledgeable you are about hockey, it's extremely difficult to be a successful coach when you don't receive solid goaltending. You have a better chance at achieving this if you are able to consider different options with input and feedback from your goaltenders.

If you're excited about learning new approaches or doing a review of the basics, you may want to jump to chapters 4 through 7 first and return to the first three chapters later. But keep in mind that you won't be able to take full advantage of the great techniques, both traditional and progressive, in chapters 4 through 7 unless you have the right equipment, the strength, and the quick reflexes you can develop by using the advice and exercises provided in chapters 1 through 3. Finally, hone your mental game by studying chapter 8.

You will likewise gain a competitive edge by using the coaches' and goalies' tips that are scattered throughout the book. Read the professional goalie profiles in each chapter that highlight players who have mastered important skills. Then study these players in action to deepen your understanding of the techniques they perform so well. The many photos in this book have been chosen carefully to illustrate proper techniques and positions, so pay close attention to them.

Continually work on your skills, improving on each aspect of your game, and learn new techniques in order to consistently improve. Commitment to becoming successful is the key to being able to advance to the next level year in and year out. In *Hockey Goaltending* I've given you the tools you need to achieve your goals. So read, study, and practice. Then put on your skates, grab your stick, and shut them out!

1

Gearing Up to Tend Goal

Available choices in goaltending equipment have grown dramatically. Equipment is lighter than in the past, designs have been improved, and you can now choose your equipment based on the way you play the game.

Don't rush your decisions. Whenever possible, experiment with different styles before you buy to determine what is the perfect fit for you. You can always order equipment to your specifications. It takes

Figure 1.1 There is a wide variety of goaltending equipment available.

a little longer, but is well worth the wait. Sometimes you may find that a local sports equipment or shoe repair shop can upgrade or repair your old equipment.

For the best prices, buy equipment after your season has ended, when sports stores are making room for new models (most manufacturers introduce their latest models in February and early March). But if you want the most up-to-date improvements, ask your dealer when he or she expects to receive an order or if he or she will order products to your specifications.

IN-LINE GOALTENDING EQUIPMENT

There is little difference between the equipment worn by pro in-line goalies and by pro ice hockey goalies. More advanced in-line hockey players use a puck that is two ounces lighter than an ice puck; some younger players use an even lighter plastic ball. Younger goaltenders playing street hockey therefore do not usually require the protection needed by professional players, and can save considerably by buying equipment specifically for in-line hockey. This equipment is not certified for ice hockey—but it is cheaper and lighter, which is better for outdoor summer hockey because it's cooler and easier to maneuver in. Anyone using a puck, however, needs equipment similar to that used for ice—even eight-year-olds sometimes play with heavy pucks!

It is essential that you know whether you will be playing with a ball or a puck. Don't turn a fun sport into a painful one by having the wrong equipment. Don't buy goalie equipment certified for ice hockey if you don't need that level of protection, because the price difference is considerable. If your equipment is too bulky, it will restrict your movement and take some of the enjoyment out of the game. Also avoid using for in-line the same equipment you play with on the ice. The hard surfaces used for in-line hockey are tough on pads and gloves and can wear down expensive equipment in a hurry.

THE STICK

Few goaltenders understand the importance of using the correct stick or the degree of variations available in a stick.

Figure 1.2   Wear the right equipment for ice or in-line hockey.

The Lie

The first thing a goalie looks at in a stick is the lie. The lie that you use depends on how you hold your blocker. The farther away your blocker is from your body, the lower the lie will be; the opposite is true if you hold the blocker close to your body. You have the correct lie when you are in your stance and the blade of your stick is lying flat on the ice. Be very careful that the lie is perfect as you are receiving the shot. Many goalies tend (incorrectly) to adjust their stance slightly just before the shot is taken—even though their stick was on the ice

Figure 1.3 Your choice of stick will affect your style and balance.

originally, their unconscious movement as the shot is released leaves the blade not in full contact with the ice.

Don't assume that the lie printed on the stick is correct. The same lie on one brand may not be identical to another. When you find the perfect stick for you, keep one as your model. When you go to buy new sticks, bring your model with you to insure that you buy an identical stick. Even as a professional with my own model, I kept a stick to insure that new batches of the same model were made to the same specifications as the old one. In fact, after using the same stick for four years, I received a shipment of four dozen sticks—all with a lower lie than on the same model used during the previous seasons! With my old stick I was able to show the company representative exactly what the mistake was.

Paddle Height

Paddle height varies greatly from one stick to another and can strongly affect the goaltender's balance. The paddle of the stick should leave the blocker at the same height as the trapper while you are in your stance. A paddle that is too short may force you to play top-heavy; a higher paddle enables you to keep your chest up and your shoulders back. Nevertheless, some goalies feel that shorter paddles allow them to keep their hands out in front of them. The most important question is whether you feel comfortable in your stance and solid on your skates.

Hold your stick at the height of your paddle. You can "doctor" the stick to fit your individual needs. If you suffer from discomfort or tendinitis between your thumb and first finger, you may want to round the edge at this point or shave the edge off with a file in order to reduce the jolt your hand takes upon impact of a shot. You also can alter the rear of the paddle, from which you actually control the stick: some goaltenders make this area thinner or make finger grooves in it so they can maintain a stronger grip.

The length of the stick determines how far you can reach out on a poke check. The current trend is toward shorter sticks, as many players feel that they can pass and stickhandle better with the shorter shaft. Playing with a high paddle doesn't require use of a high shaft and visa versa. Whether you are using a long or a short shaft, be sure that the stick is properly balanced in order to assure good control—a factor players often overlook when they modify sticks. If ordering sticks directly from the manufacturer, you can have the squared edges of the shaft rounded so it feels smoother when you slide your hand up and down the shaft.

Color

I highly recommend a light stick color so the black puck will stand out in sharp contrast to the stick. Moreover, if the stick enters the net during a save or scramble, the goal judge or referee won't be as likely to mistake part of a dark-colored stick for the puck. One option is to stick to bare wood—the color is light, and the stick will weigh a fraction less because a coat of varnish weighs less than a coat of paint.

Curve

Your selection of a curve for your stick will be highly personal. A straight blade will allow you to backhand the puck better, but will do nothing for your forehand—but keep in mind how rarely a goaltender uses a backhand. A curved stick helps you pull the puck off the boards and set it up for the defenseman; it also allows you to get height on clearing passes. The size of the curve affects the angle of the rebounds you give up, so be sure that you practice with the curve you choose.

Some goaltenders tilt their blades back slightly to get maximum height on their shots; but this can cause a fast-moving puck to jump up from the stick, and you lose control—creating more of an adventure than you want from an otherwise routine shot.

Remember, your first priority is to stop the biscuit. Being able to clear the puck and help with the breakout is important—but your choice of equipment should focus on keeping the puck out of the net.

Rocker and Heel

On the blade of a stick there is a rocker much like that of a skate. Goalie stick blades used to have no rocker at all, and no curve, thus keeping the full blade of the stick in contact with the ice. Currently available equipment permits you to increase the height of your shot and make smooth sweeping motions, by playing with less blade on the ice. Ron Hextall plays with a big rocker that enables him to get great height on his clearing passes. A goalie who has trouble lifting the puck may improve his shot dramatically by increasing his rocker. The trade-off will be a different feeling when you are in your stance with your stick on the ice. A blade in full contact with the ice lends security and balance.

When choosing a stick, pay close attention to the heel. A stick with a big rocker generally has a curved heel, while a flat blade will have a point to it or will be angled. Even a subtle change in the heel can significantly affect the balance and feel of the stick.

Do not take lightly your choice of a stick, since all the factors discussed above will affect your style and balance. Experiment whenever possible with different variations until you find the perfect stick—then stay with this make and model. Don't be afraid to doctor your stick with a file, as you may find that subtle alterations are needed to give you the perfect weapon.

The Curtis Curve

Often I am asked if the Curtis Curve is better than traditional sticks. The Curtis Curve is well-designed and innovative. Some goaltenders feel that the stick allows them to cover more of the ice surface when they lay it down, while others say that it inhibits their slide up the shaft for the poke check. In the end, you are the one who must be comfortable with your equipment, and you must decide on the basis of experimentation whether this or any other stick is right for you.

Taping Your Stick

Every hockey player likes to tape his or her stick a certain way, and goaltenders are no different. In-line goalies should tape only the face of the blade, not all the way around. It is standard practice among ice goaltenders to tape a blade from heel to toe, thereby allowing less friction and less buildup of snow when shooting the stick out. Even though taping adds a certain degree of cushion and control, some goalies avoid taping in order to prevent any affect on their blades' momentum. If it becomes a problem, you can smooth out the ridges of the tape by rubbing a puck along the blade.

Taping the handle of your stick in the area where you grab the paddle will give you more control and soften the impact of a shot. The problem with this practice is that the tape peels upward at the corners, sticking to the material of the blocker palm and making it more difficult for you to slide your blocker up the shaft. If you use this approach, remember to check the palm frequently and retape often.

The purpose of taping the knob is twofold. It should be big enough so that if you drop your stick on the ice it can be picked up easily; and it should be comfortable when you are stickhandling or sliding your blocker up for the poke check.

I highly recommend using white tape on both your blade and knob. It is easier for you to sight a black puck against a white background. When you are setting pucks for your defensemen, it also is easier for them to spot the puck off a white backdrop, facilitating their split-second reactions.

Black knobs are potentially dangerous: in a goal mouth scramble, the shaft of the goalstick may cross the goal line into the net, where the goal judge or referee might see a black object (the tape on the knob) the size of a puck entering the goal—while the real puck is actually trapped underneath the goaltender!

THE PADS

It's exciting to see the innovations and light weights in today's goalie pads. Ten years ago you did not have the selection or the decisions that you have today. There are two basic styles to choose from: one for the goaltender who likes to stand up and play a more traditional style;

and one for the person who plays the triangle and prefers to go down more often.

Materials

The traditional pad has changed in both its weight and design. Manufacturers have moved from leather to materials such as clarino and other synthetics. By replacing natural hair stuffing with foam, designers are increasing the magnitude of rebounds. If you choose to go with lightweight pads, be aware that they may make it more difficult to control your rebounds. In-line players should avoid leather pads altogether, as they simply don't last.

Not all pads slide on the ice in the same way. An inexpensive pad may not grip the ice surface sufficiently. Your goal should be to find pads that are not too heavy for you, yet whose weight does not lead to huge rebounds after the puck strikes them.

Traditional vs. Triangular

There is now a specific style of pad to accommodate goaltenders who like to butterfly and play a large triangle. The pad is more flexible and better contoured around the knee area and is designed to limit the accessibility of the five-hole. Shorter than the traditional height, it allows you to play a large triangle without restricting your movement by an overlapping of material at the top of the pad. When you switch to this pad, expect to be more comfortable performing the butter-fly—but its low cut is not for everyone.

One way of insuring a perfect fit is to order pads to your specifications. It will take longer to receive the pads, but obtaining a pair of pads that enable you to play *your* game and *your* style is well worth the delay.

Colors

If you expect to be changing teams a lot, choose a basic white or black pad—you can wear these colors with any team. Wearing white makes you look bigger on the ice, but it can start to look worn early. A dark pad may not add the illusion of size but will definitely wear for a longer period of time. If you use white pads, be aware that a colored stick will mark up the pads on the blocker side knee—so a white or nonpainted stick will be most suitable.

Straps vs. Buckles

Most goalkeepers are fussy about their equipment and the way that they wear it. A rule of thumb says that you tie the lower straps of the pad tightly to ensure control, and keep your top straps loose to cut down on the size of the rebound. Straps come with the traditional buckle or with a plastic clip. You can also combine the two—for example, use the buckle system on your lower straps and the plastic clip system on your upper straps. Although today's pads have increased protection, with a pad inside the knee covering on top, you still should wear knee pads for safety.

Fix your toe strap by looping it over, around, and through the first opening of your boot. Starting with the inside buckle already clasped allows you to secure the inside portion of your pad. Many goaltenders tire of replacing broken buckles and have begun to use laces.

Today's goaltenders are fortunate to have increased protection on the inside of the pad and the top of the knee. Don't try to save a few dollars by purchasing a pad that does not provide this essential protection. Be sure that you carefully plan your choice of pads before going to a sports store to purchase them, and always be sure that they fit you well.

THE BLOCKER

Manufacturers are working hard to improve the blocker. Much of the focus is on how the blocker should be shaped for a butterfly goaltender, or for someone who relies on the shaft-down technique. The amount of flare at the top of the glove can actually cut down the angle slightly, making it easier for you to stop the puck. The curvature allows you to lower the puck's trajectory when you redirect it, so it won't go high off the glass and take an unpredictable bounce. The flare also can help prevent the puck from squeezing between your gloves when you trap it with your glove and blocker. Some companies also are experimenting with the sides and the bottom of the blocker, to see what combinations work better for goalies.

Make sure your blocker has adequate protection around and over the fingers. This protection has become increasingly important, because goaltenders often expose their fingers as they lay their sticks along the ice. Look for some protection outside the pinkie as well as the first finger. I have twice broken this finger, which is essential in controlling the stick. You don't want your blocker to be banana-shaped, because it will expose too much of your hand; but your blocker needs some flexibility so you can lay your stick down.

Two important aspects of the blocker are the size of the palm and its placement. If the palm is too big for your hand, you will not have complete control of the blocker and will have a harder time directing rebounds. Whether the palm is of clarino or leather, it will expand somewhat when sweat and moisture build up. If the hand size is too large to begin with, in the course of play it will become even worse. Again: take your time when shopping for a blocker—a few weeks of playing with your old equipment is a small price to pay for getting something that fits you properly.

The placement of the palm has changed over the years. The palm used to be always centered in the middle of the blocker. Many current models place the palm closer to the inside, in order to reduce the overlap of blocker and pad and to cover an extra inch of unprotected space. If you have the opportunity, try gloves with different placements and decide what feels best to you. If you buy your equipment at a local sports store, be sure there is a wide range of styles from

Figure 1.4 Your choice of equipment should focus on keeping the puck out of the net.

GARTH SNOW

Vancouver Canuck goaltender Garth Snow is best known in the northeast United States as the goaltender that led the University of Maine to the 1992-93 NCAA National Championship. But a lot of NHL fans know him as the goalie with the big shoulder pads. There was a lot of discussion during the 1996-97 playoffs about the size of the equipment that Snow was using as the Philadelphia Flyers made their playoff run. This dialogue spearheaded a movement in the NHL to measure goalie equipment during the 1997-98 season, making sure that the players adhered to the league rules. Breaking the rules resulted in suspensions and fines for goaltenders. The concept that 'the bigger the equipment the goaltender uses the better chance he will have to save the puck' makes sense, but remember Snow is 6'3" and 200 pounds. If you put his equipment on Florida Panther goalie John Vanbiesbrouck's 5'8", 176 pound frame, the "Beezer" wouldn't be able to move. Goalies must chose equipment that helps them cover as much net as possible while at the same time allowing them to move comfortably.

© J. Leary/Bruce Bennett Studios

which to choose; don't hesitate to make a special order through your local store, even if it means waiting for new gear.

Although blockers often have wrist straps to hold them snugly in place, it is up to you whether or not you use the straps. If you feel better wearing your glove loose, by all means do so. But if you like your gear to feel tight, buy a blocker that has a fastening system that you can adjust to your satisfaction. If you want a strap but your present blocker doesn't have one, take your glove to your local shoe repair store and explain what you need. Goalies have long been known to doctor their equipment; you would be surprised at the things the pros do to give themselves even a slight advantage!

THE GLOVE

Today's gloves have many bells and whistles. You will find trappers with two straps for the wrist, and gloves that open up to dry more quickly after use. You can also find a glove with tackified leather on the inside, to keep your fingers from slipping. Make sure you buy a glove not because of gadgets, but because it has the proper fit, feel, size, and angle for you.

Big vs. Small

Most young goalies prefer large gloves, but with today's emphasis on the goalie's ability to handle the puck, bulkier equipment can be a hindrance. A well-selected glove permits better stickhandling and passing, and gives you more control when you drop the puck to the ice. Most goalies try to compromise by using a glove that covers maximum space without sacrificing stickhandling skills.

Pocket Angle and Palm Size

The angle at which the pocket extends from the glove differs in various models. A goalie switching from one angle to another will experience difficulty. Be sure to know your preference and stick with it. If you receive a new glove and something just doesn't feel right, check it against your old model: you may find that a slight angle change is giving you the problem.

As discussed in the blocker section, the size of the palm is extremely important. Your hand must fit properly or there may be a loss of control. Some goalies wear a batting glove to give them extra snugness, while others tape their fingers. Taping will take some of the sting away from a shot but will not decrease your sensitivity as much as a batting glove. Experiment to find out what's best for you. I always had one rule about my glove: I never let anyone else use it. I did not want to take the chance of someone with a larger hand stretching the leather and making the glove looser.

Maintenance

Early in my career I learned the importance of maintaining my glove. Keeping the shape or form is essential. You don't want to end up with a pancake pocket. Taping several pucks together and strapping them in your glove when it's not in use will help maintain the optimum pocket. Some goaltenders use a softball, a baseball, or anything else they can find to give them that perfect feel every time they slip on their glove. Don't be lazy in maintaining your equipment—it is an essential part of your ability to perform to your maximum.

Control the lacing system of the pocket before games. Don't wait until you mishandle a puck to find out that a string is loose or cut.

THE MASK

With the certification of the mask, sales of this exciting piece of equipment have gone through the roof. The number of mask manufacturers is increasing rapidly, and goalies are expressing themselves through elaborate designs. The combination of mask and cage is not a necessity for most levels, but I highly recommend it for junior, college, and pro goalies.

The advantage of the mask is that it fits snugly to your face and head, so the puck caroms off of it, spreading the shock of impact and lessening the chance of a pressure cut. Visibility is usually excellent, and the sight lines do not change throughout the game or practice due to shifting of a cage.

Because the mask is so snug, it does not breathe as well as the helmet combination. Also, because of the design, backward impact isn't as protective as that provided by a helmet. Although a mask is more expensive than a helmet cage, it is well worth the price because it reduces possible injury from high impact shots. It is not essential equipment for younger goalies because younger players don't shoot that hard.

Figure 1.5 A helmet-cage combination is fine for younger goalies. The combination of mask and cage is not a necessity for most levels of play.

For younger goaltenders the helmet-cage combination is fine. I also recommend a cage that extends over the forehead, a neck protector, and a throat guard. The chance for a young goalie to sport a painted mask like the pros may add motivation and enjoyment, but if a mask isn't in the budget he is not at risk.

The available selection of goalie masks is impressive. It's a good idea to go with proven name brands that have been on the market for many years. I would think twice about an inexpensive mask, even if superficially it appears to be as protective as established, more expensive brands. Testing procedures and degree of protection can vary greatly among manufacturers—spend a little more money and make sure that your head is protected!

The design on a mask is an expression of the goaltender and is often painted after the mask is purchased. You should be aware that a special layer of film is added at the factory after the mask has been painted. If you want to repaint the mask, you must scrape down that layer of film, apply your paint, and then reapply the film. If you are getting this work done locally be sure to have an *experienced* mask painter do all the work. You can often find one by asking other goalies or inquiring at local sports shops. Caution: once a product has been altered in any way, the manufacturer is no longer legally responsible for injuries due to the mask's failure. You may be better off ordering the mask pre-painted.

Be certain that your mask's back plate is approved for your league. For example, a pro back plate is not legal in college—so check its certification. Also various cages used at higher levels may not be acceptable in your league.

SKATES

Your choice involves not only the brand and size of the skate, but the heel and width as well. You will do best being fitted by an experienced person who understands what is needed for a perfect fit. Allow yourself time to order your specific size if necessary, as well as for an adequate period to break them in. Don't risk a poor showing by waiting until the day before tryout camp—skates don't break in overnight!

You can speed the break-in period for new leather skates by wearing damp socks your first couple of practices. If you're an ice hockey player, you may also want to try soaking your skates in the bathtub and then wearing them around the house with your skate guards on. If the skates are too stiff, skip an eyelet at the ankle area when you lace them, to leave you some bend in the ankle. Having solid, sturdy skates is so important that you should not let price be an issue when you purchase.

For in-line players, be sure to go with small wheels—the smaller the better. You'll do better with a four- or five-wheel frame. An excellent book for information about choosing in-line skates is *In-Line Skating* by Mark Powell and John Svensson.

Be aware that your feet are larger in the summer and constrict when the cold weather sets in, possibly affecting the fit of your skates. A good rule of thumb is to keep your last pair of old skates instead of discarding them, to use as replacements if something happens to your present pair.

PANTS

Equipment manufacturers have started improving every piece of equipment the goaltender wears. It is impressive to see the innova-

Figure 1.6 You will do best by being fitted for skates by an experienced person.

tions implemented in the goalie pant. Select the pant that provides adequate protection but still allows you to move comfortably. Don't use pants that are so protective you feel confined or constrained. Make sure that the inner thigh, the quadriceps, and the tailbone are protected. Also look at improvements such as a high waist area and thick padding down the outside of the hip—small benefits that nevertheless may save you three or four goals throughout the course of a season.

Some pants may come with a piece of equipment that protects the knee as well. It is not necessary to double up on protection, so if your pads already have this feature you may remove the other piece. Your pant design should give you the option of wearing suspenders and/or a belt around the waist.

CHEST PROTECTOR

The upper body is where most goaltenders are hurt from shots. That dreaded blast that catches you on the shoulder has convinced many that they would rather be shooting than receiving. Once again it is important to get adequate protection without wearing a bulky piece of equipment. Be sure your protector gives adequate protection to the collarbone area, the shoulders, and the inner arm of the glove side. The cut around the chest shouldn't be so tapered as to expose the ribs. The belly portion must extend to where the jockstrap begins; but don't go too long at this point.

If your chest protector is too bulky, you may have great protection but be too inhibited to move freely. You don't want to risk injury, but you want to play your best—so first find a piece of equipment with which you feel comfortable. If it is inadequate in a specific area, ask a local sports repair shop or shoe repairman to sew in some extra padding where you need it.

JOCK AND UNDERWEAR

One of the most painful injuries during practice occurs when a goaltender takes a shot in the groin area. If you're wearing a properly fit athletic supporter, there is no need to suffer pain caused by these shots. The protection for this area has improved immensely over the past five years, and the new models seem excellent: they use large padding that rests against the leg, leaving room so that your private parts don't touch the equipment. Do not continue with the traditional cups of the past. Women goaltenders have the option of using a jill strap—similar to a jockstrap but with a long, thin front plastic protective piece.

Many hockey players have had skin problems due to chafing from their equipment. If this is a concern, protect your skin by wearing a union suit available at most sports stores. Try to stay with a lighter material, since the containment of heat may cause premature tiredness; this problem is even worse for in-line players, for whom heat is a constant foe.

Figure 1.7   There have been improvements in every piece of equipment a goalie wears.

Many goaltenders have problems with groin pulls. If this is an area of weakness for you, wear a neoprene short under your equipment. It will keep this area warm and compact, and you will be less susceptible to strains or muscle injuries. The only drawback is the excess heat. If you get too hot, try a thin pair of spandex shorts.

Supply Bag

Figure 1.8   Every goaltender should carry his own supply bag with him.

Don't rely on your equipment manager to have everything you need. You should always stock the equipment listed below in your supply bag. If you wear a mask, you may want to consider a spare cage. Keep your last pair of skates as a backup, sharpened and ready to wear.

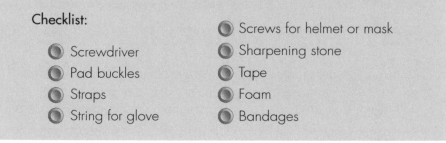

Checklist:

- Screwdriver
- Pad buckles
- Straps
- String for glove
- Screws for helmet or mask
- Sharpening stone
- Tape
- Foam
- Bandages

2

Getting Strong and Flexible

The importance of flexibility and strength for goalkeepers cannot be overemphasized. Being able to extend your body not only enables you to cover more net, it drastically cuts down on injuries. In the same way, strength makes you both a better player and one who's less likely to be hurt. Always stretch both before and after exercise, using slow, controlled (not bouncing) movements.

FLEXIBILITY TRAINING

Before practice or games, work up a sweat by going for a short run or riding the stationary bike. Anywhere from 8 to 15 minutes should be ample time to get a good sweat going before taking a few minutes to stretch your thighs, hamstrings, calves, and back muscles. Once on the ice, perform a few stretches after several laps around the rink in order to stay loose.

After practice or a game, find a spot to stretch for another 10 minutes or so; this will allow you to recover more quickly and maintain your improved flexibility. If you are serious about staying injury-free and improving your game, consult a trainer for a complete stretching program tailored to your specific needs.

Stretches With a Teammate

You can concentrate on five specific stretches, to be done with a teammate. These stretches will not only maintain your flexibility, but will improve it. For the stretches to be effective and safe, be sure that your partner understands the goal of each exercise. She should not try to hold you while you work against her resistance. Only enough pressure should be applied to make you work in a smooth and controlled motion, avoiding any bouncing or sudden movements.

PARTNER-RESISTED SEATED STRAIGHT LEG

Sit on the floor with your legs extended straight out in front of you. With a teammate gently applying pressure from behind, lean forward as far as possible while keeping your back straight. When you have reached maximum extension, slowly return to the upright position as your partner resists. Perform this sequence several times; you should be able to extend farther with each stretch. A slight variation to this exercise is to spread your legs out forming a "V".

PARTNER-RESISTED LEG RAISES

Lie flat on your back with your legs straight. Your teammate should brace one leg with his or her hand above your knee. Raise the other leg as far as possible off the floor without bending your knee. When you cannot raise it any further, contract your hamstring and push downward against your teammate's resistance. Perform this stretch several times using both legs and you will find that you have a greater range of motion each time.

PARTNER-RESISTED LEG FLEXION

Lie flat on your stomach with arms and legs completely extended. Your partner should hold your hips down with one hand, while placing his other hand under one knee. With your partner's help, slowly raise your leg as far as you are comfortable, then contract your muscles and force the leg back to the ground against your partner's resistance in a slow and controlled manner. Repeat four or five times with each leg, attempting to raise your leg further each time.

PARTNER-RESISTED BUTTERFLY GROIN STRETCH

In a seated position, join the soles of your feet forming a diamond with your legs. Have a partner place the palm of his hands on your knees as he faces you. Release your legs toward the ground by relaxing the muscles and yielding to gentle downward pressure applied by your teammate. Stop at maximum extension and squeeze your legs together against the resistance of your partner. Perform this exercise several times, always attempting to get closer to the ground.

PARTNER-RESISTED LOW BACK PRESS

Standing erect on both feet, bend at the waist until your trunk is parallel to the ground. Do not lock your knees. Have a teammate place his hands on your shoulders while facing you. With your partner's help, bend over as far as possible in the direction of your toes. When you are bent over as far as possible, raise your trunk in a slow and controlled manner while your partner resists. With each repetition (four or five), try to extend past your original maximum stretch.

Individual Stretches

You will not always have someone available to help you stretch. When this is the case, perform the following 10 simple stretches on your own. You may also do them in conjunction with the partner stretches.

CALF STRETCH

Leaning against a wall, extend your legs while balancing your weight on the balls of your feet. Slowly press each heel toward the ground alternately, stretching the calf muscle of both legs.

PRONE QUADRICEPS STRETCH

While lying flat on your stomach, bend your right leg and grab your ankle. Pull your leg up and back, getting a full stretch of the thigh muscle. Reverse legs.

SEATED STRAIGHT LEG

Sitting on the floor with your legs extended forward, lower your chest toward your knees while bending slowly at the waist. Full extension of the stretch can be achieved by holding your calves and pulling your torso forward. Remember that smooth and steady movement is essential.

INVERTED HURDLER PROGRESSION: PRETZEL

Sitting up, as in the previous exercise, bend your right knee forming a 90-degree angle and cross it over the left leg, which remains flat on the ground. With your left elbow, press against the outside of your right knee, rotating your torso to the right. You should feel the stretch in your hips and lower back. Alternate legs.

BUTTERFLY GROIN STRETCH

From a sitting position on the floor, bend both legs so that the soles of your feet are touching, forming a diamond with your legs. Place your forearms over your knees. Relax the groin area and stretch by slowly pushing down with your forearms. Ideally, your knees will touch the floor. When you've stretched as far as you can, contract these muscles by pulling your knees up toward you against the resistance of your arms, just as you did in the hamstring stretch. Relax for a few minutes, then try the stretch again. You should be able to stretch further this time.

PRONE ABDOMINAL STRETCH

Lying flat on your stomach, place your hands in position to do a push-up. Using only your arms, lift your upper body off the ground while keeping your hips in contact with the floor, arching your back. After your arms are extended as far as possible, hold the stretch for a few seconds; then slowly lower yourself. This exercise stretches the lower back area.

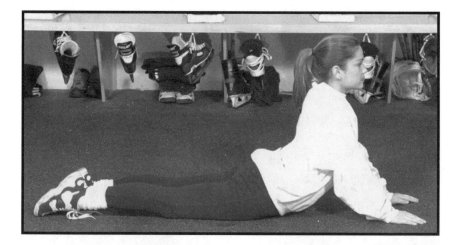

MAD CAT ARCH

Get on your hands and knees. Push the middle of your back toward the ceiling, hold for 10 seconds, then bring it back down.

SHOULDER STRETCH

Stand upright. With your right hand, pull your left elbow inward toward your chest, thus stretching your shoulder muscles. Alternate arms.

SIDE STRETCH

To stretch your lats (upper back), raise your right hand and arm to the ceiling. Without rotating your hips, bend at the waist and let the upper body fall to the left hand side. Repeat with left arm.

NECK ROTATION

Standing erect, place hands on hips. Slowly rotate your head in large circular movements in the right direction and then the left. Do not rotate your head backward. Experience the stretch in your neck and shoulders.

AEROBIC AND ANAEROBIC CAPACITY

There is no way you can perform at your peak without being in top physical condition. Essential elements to competing at your highest level are aerobic/anaerobic capacity and muscle strength.

Never go into training camp hoping that the tryout process will get you into shape. Without your muscles being able to recover quickly, and without the capacity to take in sufficient oxygen and to use it efficiently, you will not be able to perform at your best. Entering training camp unprepared will lead to a slow start to the season and disappointment in the eyes of the coaching staff. Have respect for yourself, your coaches, and teammates by showing up the first day of hockey ready to perform. During the season you should be concerned with maintaining the peak condition achieved in the off-season.

Aerobic Training

Years ago coaches stressed the importance of running to increase aerobic endurance; but today there are many ways to improve your aerobic capacity. Of course running is one of them—but I question the physical benefits of such pounding on your knees. Technology has improved so much in stationary bikes, stair climbers, rowing machines, and climbing machines, that they all make excellent alternatives. Improving aerobic capacity is a task you should do *off* the ice, because exercising on the ice while fatigued negatively affects your skill and fundamentals. For more information on building aerobic strength, see Peter Twist's *Complete Conditioning for Ice Hockey*, published by Human Kinetics.

Anaerobic Training

Sprints, plyometrics, and interval training are excellent methods by which to increase your anaerobic threshold. The key while training in this manner is maximum effort for a short period (e.g., 10 seconds) with a rest of approximately three times the length of the exercise (e.g., 30 seconds of rest between 10-second bouts). The closer you get to the season, the more you should concentrate on anaerobic training. Spend the first few months after your season is over to emphasize aerobic training, and the period after that to increase strength.

I believe an excellent training regimen for goaltenders is to compete in sports such as handball, racquetball, and squash. Racquet sports demand that you utilize a low stance and explode out of that stance, making split-second decisions; you must follow a small object moving at fast speeds, and intercept that object using hand-eye coordination. These high intensity games force the players to concentrate over long periods but with frequent pauses. Another helpful pursuit is to learn to juggle, an activity that demands the most rigorous and instantaneous hand-eye coordination.

In the late 1980s, "cross-training" referred to athletes' practice of competing in numerous different sports. It can still mean that now. However, cross-training can also refer to general conditioning—not necessarily competing—in several sports. For goalies, cross-training is a great way to break up your week by playing different sports and using a variety of training approaches to achieve your goals. Make working out and improving your game fun! Do not get stuck in boring routines that lower your level of enthusiasm and thus your improvement as an athlete.

STRENGTH TRAINING

Weight training is a controversial subject for goaltenders. Some swear by it and others swear against it. I believe that muscle strength is essential to maximizing a goalie's potential. The more power you have available, the quicker you can explode from one point to the other. You must also be able to maintain your positioning around the crease area and not be manhandled easily by opponents. When you are approaching the playoffs, you want to be physically strong and not weakened by the demands of the season.

A common myth is that weight training will give you big muscles and decrease your flexibility. Not true. By using lower weights and higher repetitions you can increase your strength and power significantly without looking like the guys on the front of bodybuilding magazines. Be smart: use weight training to add to your muscular conditioning and strength. Consult an expert to obtain a custom program devoted to improving on your weaknesses. Learn how to use the equipment properly and how to maximize your efforts. Again, *Complete Conditioning for Ice Hockey* is an excellent resource in this area for both ice and in-line goaltenders.

Free Weights vs. Machines

Some goalies prefer free weights, and others like machines. Both have their advantages, and both methods work. Free weights stress the connective tissue and surrounding muscles in addition to your target muscle. Machines are better at isolating muscles because they keep your body in one place, which takes away the need to balance the weight and cuts down on your ability to cheat. Machines can also be safer, and they can save you a lot of time setting up and taking down equipment. I recommend that my goalies use a combination of the two. When using light weights, dumbbells and barbells are fine— but when you tackle heavier weights, be smart and use a machine.

Exercises

There are plenty of exercises that will benefit goaltenders and can be done individually, or combined with a weightlifting program. Yet not everyone has the time or resources to use a gym. Below I have listed eight exercises that can be done at home and can have a major effect on your game.

CALF RAISES

Stand on a step or block with your arms balancing your weight and feet close together. Place the balls of your feet at the edge of the step and drop your left heel toward the ground while raising your right foot off the step. At its maximum stretch, concentrate on the calf muscle to pull your body weight as high as possible. Repeat this until you feel the burn in your muscle; then switch sides. Repeat each set three times.

LUNGES

Standing straight, take an exaggerated step forward with one foot, so the angle at your knee is approximately 90 degrees. Control your balance in this lunged state, then perform the same movement with the other foot. Continue making steps until you tire and find it hard to maintain your balance. Take a 45-second break and repeat the exercise.

For a variation of this exercise, use a chair positioned behind you to support your back leg. Start in the lunge position with your front leg bent, and your back foot resting on the chair. As you straighten out your front leg, lift your heel off the floor so you're standing on the ball of your foot—this works your calf muscle as well. Keep the calf flexed for three seconds, then lower your heel back to the floor.

SQUATS

Stand with your back against a wall and with your feet about the same distance from the wall as your knee is from your hip. Slide your back downward until your thighs and torso form a 90-degree angle. Hold this position as long as possible without using your hands to support any weight. Take a 45-second break, shake your legs out, and try again, always challenging yourself to hold on longer than the last time.

SIDE LEG RAISES

Lie on your left side. Support your head with your left arm and lift your right leg as high as possible without any rotation or bend, then bring it back down again. Continue this up-and-down motion until you can do no more. At the point of exhaustion, bend your right knee to 90 degrees, and let it rest behind your left leg, with your right foot touching the floor. Lift the left leg as high as possible by contracting the inner thigh of your left leg. Repeat to exhaustion. Complete three sets of this exercise, then switch sides.

You should do no more than 100 repetitions of either of these movements. If you can do more than 100, use a weight at the end of your foot or have a teammate provide resistance in order to bring your exhaustion point below 100.

PRONE LEG RAISES

Lying flat on your stomach, extend your body fully. Keeping your right leg straight, extend it as high as possible. Slowly raise and lower the right leg, while your left leg stays in contact with the floor. Repeat this movement until exhaustion, then change legs. Repeat this exercise three times.

Do no more than 100 repetitions of this exercise. If you can do more, use a weight at the end of your foot or have a teammate provide resistance.

PUSH-UPS

Lying on your stomach, place your hands slightly farther than shoulder-width apart. Keeping your body rigid, push your entire body up, contracting your chest, triceps, and shoulder muscles. Do as many push-ups as possible, then rest for 45 seconds. Complete four sets of push-ups.

TRICEPS DIPS

Having power in your triceps will increase your recovery time immensely. When returning to your feet from your backside, you typically will call upon the triceps to spring you up.

Set two chairs, facing each other, about 4 feet apart. With your back to one chair, place your hands on its seat while placing the heels of your feet on the other chair seat. Hold the weight of your body by fully extending your arms. From this position, dip your rear toward the floor while maintaining control with the triceps. Finally, power your weight back to the initial starting position. Repeat to the point of exhaustion. After resting a short time, complete another two sets—each consisting of repetition to exhaustion and separated by a period of rest of approximately two minutes.

CRUNCHES

Lie on your back with your calves on the seat of a chair. Your legs should form a 90-degree angle. Keeping your lower back pressed against the floor, raise your chest toward your knees. Once your abdominal muscles have contracted and brought your chest as far forward as possible, hold the position for three seconds, then relax. After you have performed as many repetitions as possible, pause for 45 seconds and repeat three more sets.

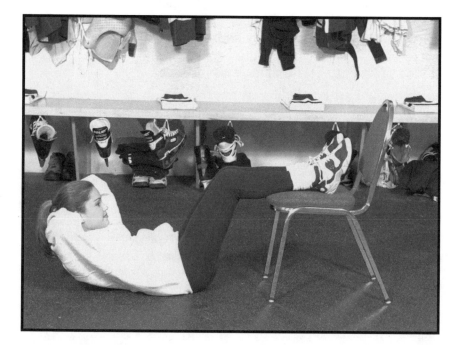

THE GAME WARM-UP

A good warm-up is essential for a productive practice or a successful game. You should take it upon yourself to be prepared when you hit the ice—and, when necessary, to explain your needs to a coach who may not be knowledgeable about the importance of warm-ups. Be tactful. Choose a convenient time when you and the other goalkeepers can sit down with the coach and discuss the issue. Be willing to listen, but also be firm on what you need, and try to come to a mutual understanding on what is best for the goalies and the team.

Practice

Your warm-up should begin well before your practice begins. Arrive at the rink a few minutes early and go for a run or ride the stationary bike if there is one available. After you have raised your heart rate and broken into a sweat, go through your stretching routine before you get dressed. Time in the rink is limited, so you don't want to spend 15 minutes out there getting loosened up. Once on the rink, skate a few good laps and perform some stretches before you get ready to play.

Although not always possible, ideally you should have an individual shooter warm you up. If you do have the chance, set a player in the high slot with a bunch of pucks. Have her shoot to each of the four corners about 15 times. Your goal is to concentrate, and get a feel for the puck. Have her take good honest shots, not too slow but not blasts either. Get in a good rhythm with the shooter; this is not a rapid-fire exercise.

Regardless of whether the goaltender has had an individual warm-up, the first couple of drills should be set up for his benefit. Shots should be taken from just inside the blue line, preferably snap or wrist shots, and off center (absolutely no deking). This should give the goalie a high save percentage and allow him to get in a groove of performing the correct saves and making special effort to control rebounds. If the coach sets up drills specifically for your benefit, don't insult her by being lazy. This is a perfect chance for you to work on your skills.

Game

The goaltender should always perform an off-ice warm-up before a game. He should also have a warm-up after he gets onto the ice. The pregame on-ice warm-up should comprise the following four parts:

1. Individual shooter
2. Long off-angle shots
3. Team situations, 2-1, 3-2 with breakout
4. Mid-range rapid-fire snap shots

The main purpose of the warm-up should be to get the goaltender ready for the game. Drills that have the shooters blasting from close range, making three passes in front of the goal mouth, or deking are detrimental to the goalie's preparation.

Stay away from drills that give high percentages to the shooter. This would include 2-on-0 and breakaways. Getting beaten on four consecutive breakaways in warm-up can change a goalie's mental state and take away some of her aggressiveness. The players should be shooting "for the goaltender" the majority of warm-up.

The backup goaltender must understand the starter's needs. Some goalies like to see a ton of rubber before a game, while others want to feel fresh and rested. The starter should have the liberty of moving in and out of the net as he pleases.

It is a good idea to check that the net has been placed in the correct position. Often, because of poor ice conditions or insufficient training, the net may be drilled off center, causing you to be off your angle even when you are positioned properly. You can also check this before each period, and notify the officials if the net is off center.

INJURIES

Because of the physical demands placed on goaltenders, injuries are a major concern. There is often a lot of pressure to return to play as quickly as possible after an injury; this quick return is often viewed as toughness and dedication to the team. It is important to remember

TOM BARRASSO

Tom Barrasso is the first American-born NHL goaltender to reach the 300-win plateau. Unfortunately, because of shoulder surgery, he was only able to play 5 games in the 1996-97 campaign. Barrasso has fought back to recapture his form and claim the number one job with the Pittsburgh Penguins, the team with whom he won two Stanley Cups. Here is a goalie who missed 95 percent of an entire season at 31 years old and was able to come back, regain his form, and be considered one of the top goalies in the NHL. If you're worried that taking the time needed to overcome an injury will cause you to lose your spot on the team or that the team will suffer without you, think twice. Coming back to the team completely healthy will make you a much greater asset than if you tried to come back before you were ready to play. You only hurt yourself and the team if you try to play while you're hurt or sick.

© Bruce Bennett Studios

that it will be you who pays the price down the road and not your coaches or teammates. Sometimes it is hard to consider the future when the present is the most important thing in your life, but mature decisions can make the difference between a short and a long career.

After an injury, it is essential to get the best diagnosis possible. Don't be shy about getting second and third opinions. Seek out the most qualified specialist: the importance of finding the best doctors cannot be overemphasized. Make sure that the team is well informed of the diagnosis and understands the worst possible scenario as well as the best. Plan on the longest possible recovery time, and simply be grateful if you can return earlier than that.

Never return before an injury is 100 percent healed and your strength has returned to at least 85 percent of previous maximum. Many goaltenders who return from groin and knee injuries have learned the hard way about coming back too soon. Proper rehabilitation is essential to a full recovery. Make sure you are treated by a sports therapist familiar with the demanding movements of a goalie. Do not stop therapy the minute you return to the rink; ease into practice sessions while continuing your therapy.

Most important of all, do not let someone else say you must return to play. You know your body better than anyone. When you are confident that it is time to return and your doctor is in agreement, then and only then should you return to the goal. You make the call!

3

Improving Speed and Quickness

Everyone would like to have the natural athletic ability of a Michael Jordan or Deion Sanders. There is a misconception that athletic ability is God-given and cannot be improved upon. Mike Duffy, as a conductor of speed, agility, and quickness sports camps throughout the country, has worked with professional and amateur athletes in all sports and has made a living disproving this idea.

MIKE DUFFY'S SPEED, AGILITY, AND QUICKNESS TRAINING

Duffy has designed a program specifically for goaltenders to improve speed, quickness, and agility. Along with Mike's program, I have included drills that can increase foot speed and tennis ball drills that will improve hand-eye coordination and balance. Drills alone, however, won't suffice: get involved as much as possible in non-hockey activities that will help your game during the off-season. After the age of fifteen, summer hockey is a must, but don't neglect other sports. Exercising your mind and body in different capacities will greatly improve your abilities as a goaltender.

Foot Speed Drills

Increasing a goalie's foot speed will dramatically improve his or her game. This is why I recommend sports such as squash and racquetball because they force you to execute short, quick strides. Although running improves your aerobic capacity, those long methodical strides do nothing for foot speed. Below are five drills to increase your quickness.

SPRINTS

After a good warm-up, complete a series of sprints or dashes. Start with a 100-yard sprint and subtract 20 yards after each sprint; jog easily back to your starting position. Concentrate on your explosion: pulling your feet in under you as quickly as possible as you accelerate. After you have completed one set of sprints, perform some stretches before resuming. After completing your forward sprints, repeat the same exercise only backward.

CROSSOVERS

Instead of facing the point you are sprinting to, turn sideways to the left. Generate speed by crossing your left leg in front of your right and plant your foot. Your second stride should be made with your right leg and next your left should follow, crossing behind the right. Remain facing sideways throughout the entire sprint and work in both directions.

UPHILL SPRINTS

An excellent way to develop quick feet is to sprint uphill. Concentrate on short powerful strides, generating as much speed as possible.

SKIPPING ROPE

Long, looping swings of the rope for longer duration will help with conditioning but not speed. Use a combination of regular rhythm with short bursts of frantic pace—just as action comes and goes when you are in the net.

STAIRS

Running up stairs is a great way to work on speed and quadriceps muscles. You can do this indoors or out. Exercises like this one will prove their worth in the final minutes of a game when you're dead tired and your team is counting on you to hold the lead or keep them in the game.

Mike Duffy's Training Principles

As is true with other aspects of athleticism, speed, agility, and quickness can be enhanced through proper training and conditioning. Just as weight training may help an athlete to reach better performance levels, speed, agility, and quickness training will help an athlete to achieve better results in any sport where such qualities affect performance. A person whose genetic makeup is that of a long-distance runner can lift weights forever in any type of training regimen, but the person will never look like Arnold Schwarzenegger. To look like Arnold one must have a certain genetic makeup on top of the re-quired thousands of hours of work and exercise. However, no matter what body type you have, weight training will improve your strength and help you come closer to reaching your full athletic potential.

The same can be said for speed, agility, and quickness (SAQ) training. You can do all of the speed drills and exercises in the world, but you are never going to be as fast as Carl Lewis unless you have his genetic potential. However, by going through all of the speed drills, you will definitely become faster and quicker, moving closer to your genetic potential and improving your athletic performance.

SAQ training is a relatively new field in sport science. It is generally recognized that motor learning and development can be enhanced through practice of a variety of coordination activities ranging from simple to complex to highly complex. Hand-to-eye coordination and foot-to-eye coordination (and a myriad of other body part-to-body part coordination) activities help athletes develop more fluid and graceful body movement, with concomitant improvements in performance. SAQ training has taken this concept one step further by saying that, with the same type of practice, you can also enhance the speed with which those motor skills are performed.

ESSENTIAL SAQ TRAINING CONCEPTS

If you do not understand the underlying concepts of SAQ training, and therefore perform the drills incorrectly, you will be permanently programming the wrong movements into your body and your brain. The concepts are as follows:

CONCEPT 1: Explosive Power for Speed Comes From the Balls of the Feet. You can prove this to yourself very quickly. Stand up and put all of your weight on your heels, and pick the balls of your feet up off the floor. Then try to jump into the air as high as you can. After you've tried this a couple of times, try jumping from the balls of your feet with the heel off the ground. Which method allows you to be more explosive?

The point of this concept is that you want to avoid having the heel hit the ground while going through these drills and exercises. Furthermore, the more time your foot spends on the ground, the slower you are going to be. If your heel strikes the ground, you are not moving as fast as you can. Since you get no explosive power for speed from your heels, why would you ever want them to touch the ground when you're training for speed and quickness?

CONCEPT 2: Explosive Power for Speed Increases With Increases in Stored Energy. Explosive power occurs when the ball of the foot pushes off the ground. There are two biomechanical, technical definitions that you need to understand to grasp this concept. The first of these is *dorsiflexion*. Put simply, dorsiflexion is the movement of the foot and ankle in which the toes are flexed up. *Plantar flexion* is the movement of the foot and ankle when the toes point down.

The foot pushing off the ground in plantar flexion releases energy that is stored in the muscles of the calf, leading to explosive speed. This release of energy occurs when the foot moves from dorsiflexion to plantar flexion. The muscles of the lower leg are storing energy during the time that the foot is in dorsiflexion. They release that energy when the foot moves to the plantar flexion. The more energy you can store in the calf muscles during dorsiflexion, the more explosive the push-off will be. You should try to get your foot back to dorsiflexion as quickly as possible after the plantar flexion action of push-off. The simple reminder "Knee up, heel up, toe up" should help you to practice proper lower body mechanics for explosive speed.

CONCEPT 3: Fast Hands Equal Fast Feet, and Fast Feet Equal Fast Hands. Once again, you can prove this to yourself easily. Stand up and jog in place, using your arms in a manner similar to regular running. Once you've established a standard, comfortable pace, try speeding up your hands and arms, while keeping your legs and feet at the same pace. You should find that it is all but impossible to do this without changing the amount of swing in your arms. Do the same thing again, this time running in place at a considerably faster rate than your jog. Try to slow down your arms and hands, while keeping your feet moving at the same fast pace. Once again, you should find it impossible to do without changing your arm swing.

The point of this concept is for you to realize that your upper body is just as important to speed development as your lower body. It is important to practice good arm mechanics at all times during SAQ training.

You may not know the proper arm mechanics for maximum speed. So as part of this concept, you'll find four simple rules that will allow you to get the most out of your upper body for speed development.

1. ***Keep your arms at a 90-degree angle.*** Short levers move faster than long levers. Think about the pendulum on a grandfather clock. If the clock has a long arm, how fast does it move? If the clock has a short arm, how fast does it move? The shorter the arm, the faster it moves. The same is true for your arm. It will move faster when it is shorter. Keep your arms bent 90 degrees and swing from the shoulder. Many athletes swing from the elbow, which is incorrect. When you swing from the elbow you lengthen your lever, slowing down your arms and consequently slowing your feet.

2. ***Swing your arms so that the hands move from chest to butt.*** You want your swing to be short and compact. Chest to butt is ideal. How many world class sprinters do you see who swing their arms over their head? They keep their arm swing short and compact. The emphasis should be on chest (first) to butt (second). Try this: put both your hands down by your hips. Swing them as hard as you can up to your chest. Which way does this propel your body? Now try holding your hands out and swing them as hard as you can down to your hips. Which way does this propel your body? If you're doing this right you should see that when you swing your arms from the chest down, it propels your body forward, which is the way you want to go anyway. If you swing the arm down from chest to butt, your body will naturally take care of getting back from the butt to the chest.

3. ***Keep your hands outside of your eyes.*** Any time your hands cross your eyes from one side or the other, your upper body ceases to move in a straight line and starts to move slightly from side to side. This is known as *rotational movement*. Rotational movement not only slows you down, but it requires more energy than linear movement, which affects your stamina. Think of it this way: you've heard that the shortest distance between two points is a straight line. Make your body move in that same straight line to get between those two points as quickly as possible.

4. ***Brush your pinkies against your pockets.*** This reinforces the principles discussed in rule 3. You may occasionally see people who run very awkwardly with their arms swinging from side to side, yet their hands never cross their eyes. Those people are still hampered by rotational movement. Rule 4 is especially for those people. You will find that if you brush your pinkies past your pants pockets while you're running, you can all but eliminate rotational movement.

These are the four basic rules of upper body mechanics for speed development. If you do nothing else but concentrate on these four things, you will probably improve your speed and quickness to a limited extent. One other important thing to remember (it should really be a fifth rule) is to relax, relax, relax. Tight muscles do not move quickly. If your hands are tight, the odds are that the rest of the muscles in your arms will be tight also. Once the muscles in the shoulders tighten up, the levers move more slowly and your speed decreases. Pretend that you are holding baby birds in your hands when you're running. Don't let the bird get away, but don't crush it either. Holding your hands like this will help the muscles of your upper body to remain loose.

Dynamic Flexibility Drills

Dynamic flexibility is an excellent way to warm up, because it gets blood flowing to the muscles with gentle stretching rather than with shocking movements that can injure a cold muscle. It is already practiced at various levels by many college and professional teams. How often do you stretch in a stationary position during competition? Probably not often. Most of us generally stretch while in motion or "dynamically." It is quite possible that in the next few years, static stretching will become all but obsolete, because dynamic flexibility programs are much more effective.

There are three goals to a flexibility program:

1. **Warm the muscle.** Your muscles are like rubber bands. What would happen if you took a rubber band, threw it in a freezer for a couple of hours, then tried to stretch it right after it came out of the freezer? It would snap right in half! I've exaggerated my point, but the lesson is that you never want to stretch the muscles before warming them up.

2. **Stretch the muscle.** This goal is usually attained through the static stretching part of a warm-up. However, wouldn't it be better if you stretch a muscle the way it needs to be stretched during competition?

3. **Educate the muscle.** Ideally, at the same time that we are warming and stretching a muscle, we would like to teach it how to react during competition. This is especially true for the development of speed, agility, and quickness.

DOMINIK HASEK

During my second season playing professionally in Switzerland, we played a preseason game against the Czech club Dukla Jihivala. A teammate pulled me out of the locker room to watch their goalie, Dominik Hasek, during their morning pregame skate. While we stood watching, he told me that Hasek was regarded as the best goaltender in Europe. My first response was that because of his unique style he probably would be kicked out of goalie school! His style has been likened to someone frantically looking for their lost contact lenses on the ground. We played Dukla the evening after I had picked his game apart during that morning skate — and Hasek shut us out. What I remember most was that despite his style, Hasek's quickness was unbelievable for such a tall goalie. He has won the Hart Trophy as the NHL's most valuable player, the Vezina Trophy as the NHL's best goaltender, and back-stopped the Czech Republic to a Gold medal at the 1998 Winter Olympics in Nagano. His remarkable quickness and outstanding athletic ability make him one of the best goalies in the world.

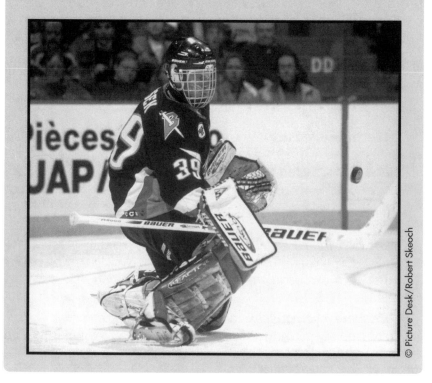

© Picture Desk/Robert Skeoch

SKIPPING DRILLS AND DYNAMIC MOVEMENTS

The following skipping drills and dynamic movements will enable you to warm, stretch, and educate your muscles in a manner that will enhance speed development. The drills can easily be done in a 10- to 15-minute period.

Take a few minutes after completing these drills to further stretch any muscles that you feel need more attention or that still have not been adequately stretched. For best results, do these drills in the order given. Although the length of time you spend skipping should vary by sport, 10-20 minutes generally should be sufficient for each exercise. Whatever distance you decide upon, split the distance in half. During the first half, work on being explosive in your skip and using as much range of motion as possible, so as to get a good dynamic stretch. During the second half, concentrate on speed. Speed in this case does not mean moving from point A to point B as fast as possible, but rather moving your feet quickly with as many foot strikes (foot hitting the ground) as possible between points A and B.

Skipping drills are excellent as part of a dynamic flexibility routine, because they accomplish the routine's three basic objectives. The very act of skipping, for example, educates the muscles in quick, balanced foot interaction with the ground. As you go through these drills, make yourself practice the proper fundamental mechanics. Concentrate on the four basic rules of upper body movement that were stated previously; concentrate especially on good foot interaction with the ground and on keeping the "knee up, heel up, toe up" position as much as possible throughout your skip.

ANKLE FLIP SKIP

Throughout this drill, try to keep both legs straight. Start on the ball of your right foot and bounce on it twice. Jump forward and land on the left foot, then bounce on it twice. Keep going forward while alternating between the left and the right feet. Try jumping farther and farther; emphasize the explosion off the ball of your foot so that you work the muscles of the lower calf. Go forward for about 30 seconds, then turn around and come back.

HEEL TO BUTT SKIP

Bring the heel of one leg to your rear end (knee pointing down) as you bounce twice off the other leg. Alternate legs, and try to kick yourself in the butt as you do this drill.

DEAD LEG SKIP

Skip forward on one leg and do high knee lifts with the other, hopping twice for each knee lift. Pump your arms forward and try to lift the knee as high as possible. Go in one direction for 5-10 seconds, then turn around and switch legs.

DOUBLE LEG SKIP

Skip on alternate legs using good knee lift for both legs. If you want, you may do arm circles (arms circle in a swimming motion) during this skip to begin some upper body dynamic flexibility. Don't worry about which arm should be going forward with which leg, just let it be natural. Even if you don't wish to do the arm circles, concentrate on good arm mechanics.

KARATE KICK SKIP

This is just like the Double Leg Skip, except you should kick the leg straight out in front of you, karate style, after the initial knee lift. Bounce twice off the foot in the non-kicking leg while going through the kicking motion. This will look and feel awkward at first. Be sure that you get good knee lift before karate kicking the leg out in front of you.

CHICKEN SCRATCH SKIP

This is similar to the Karate Kick Skip except now you should emphasize the downward snap of the leg after the karate kick. The motion should be like a chicken scratching the ground, or a bull pawing at the ground before charging. It is still important to get good knee lift. Your foot should be almost directly beneath your hip when it hits the ground on this skip. Again, you should be bouncing off the non-kicking leg twice during the kicking/scratching motion.

WIDE SKIP

Follow the actions of the Double Leg Skip, but after bringing your knee straight up, work on hip flexibility by taking the knee out to the side before replanting. You can use a side-to-side arm action here if you want.

LUNGE WALK

By this time you should be at least slightly warm and breathing harder than normal. Slow down with the lunge walk to stretch the hip flexors. Stride out farther than your normal stride. Thrust the hips down and forward, nearly touching your trailing knee to the ground. Come back to a balanced position and stride out with the opposite leg.

RUSSIAN MARCH WALK/SKIP

You can walk or skip for this exercise, depending on your skill level and how you feel. Hold your hands out in front of you at about shoulder height. Try to kick yourself in the hands as you walk or skip to your destination point.

SIDE STRADDLE SKIP

Bounce twice off your right foot, then quickly step to your left. Bounce twice off your left foot while pulling your right leg back under your body. Repeat the sequence by bouncing twice on your right foot (stepping directly down rather than moving either right or left), then stepping sideways with your left foot, and so on, for about 30 seconds. Flex at the knee and the hip throughout this drill. When you finish in one direction, switch legs and come back facing the same way so that you work both legs equally.

CROSSOVER SKIP

Moving sideways as you did in the Side Straddle Skip, cross the trail leg over the lead leg and skip. The original lead leg then steps behind the trail leg back into the lead position (only the trail leg crosses over). Each foot will bounce off the ground twice before the other foot strikes the ground. Try to get your shoulders to move with your hips as much as possible, without losing balance. When you reach your destination point, come back facing the same way so that you work on each leg equally.

SKIPPIOCA

This is a short skipping version of the Carioca drill. Start as you did the Crossover Skip. The trail leg will cross in front of the lead leg and bounce twice. The original lead leg then steps back to the original starting position and bounces twice. The trail leg then crosses behind the lead leg and bounces twice. The lead leg completes the cycle by stepping in front of the trail leg to the original position and starting over. Unlike in the Crossover Skip, try to keep the shoulders as square as possible during the drill. As with all the other side movement drills, when you reach your destination point, come back facing the same way so that you work on each leg equally.

DROP STEP SKIP

This final skip will help you become more proficient at one of the most underdeveloped skills in athletics. Start with your back facing your destination point. Rotate 90 degrees to either side, and step with that leg toward the destination point, so that one shoulder is now pointing at your destination point. Bounce off that foot twice and rotate 180 degrees backward, so that the other foot and shoulder move toward the destination point. Bounce off that foot twice and repeat the drop step with another 180-degree pivot to your back side. Practice throwing the elbow hard past your hip as you drop step.

JUGGLING

Perhaps the funniest day of goaltender camp is when I teach everyone to juggle. It takes 90 percent of the goalies less than 30 minutes to learn how to juggle three balls; they spend the rest of the day juggling anything they can get their hands on.

Basic Juggling

Take your time and carefully follow the instructions below to learn the basic steps of juggling. Don't jump ahead until you can execute each step perfectly.

STEP 1 FOR LEARNING TO JUGGLE

Standing erect, hold a tennis ball in your throwing hand (for most this is the right hand). Place your elbows to your sides, with your

forearms out in front of your body and parallel to the ground. Using your wrist, toss the tennis ball underhand to your left hand, creating a high arc. This arc should pass just over your forehead. Catch the ball with your left hand and place it once again in your right. Do not toss the ball with your left hand—at this point we are perfecting only the right toss. After you feel comfortable with throwing the ball with your right hand, repeat the process with your left. Spend a minimum of 10 minutes perfecting your style.

STEP 2 FOR LEARNING TO JUGGLE

Place a second ball in your left hand. Toss the ball that's in your right hand toward your left. As it reaches the top of the arc, toss the

second ball *inside* the path of the first. Catch the balls and stop. Repeat the exercise again, throwing the right ball first, until you are comfortable. The most common mistake at this point is to rush the second ball. It may help to count "one and two and . . ." to help with your rhythm.

STEP 3 FOR LEARNING TO JUGGLE

Once you have perfected step 2, place a third ball in your right hand along with the first ball. Rest one ball on two fingers, with the other in your palm. Do the same exercise as in the last drill, but with one extra throw. Toss one of the balls from the right hand toward your left. As the ball hits the peak, toss the ball from your left to right. As

that ball hits its peak, you should have caught the first ball (with your left hand) and be throwing the third (from your right hand). You'll end with one ball in your right hand and two in your left. Make no more than these three tosses until you can consistently control all three balls. Now, place one of the balls you have in your left hand into your right and repeat the sequence.

STEP 4 FOR LEARNING TO JUGGLE

If you can complete the last step, you are ready to juggle. Simply follow the last instructions, but continue by throwing for a second time with your left hand. Count how many throws you can make before you lose control. It won't be long until you're juggling naturally.

Once you've learned the basic skills, you can try different techniques. Try juggling objects of different weight, or throwing the balls outside your hands instead of inside, or even behind your back.

TWO BALL JUGGLE

A great way to work on your catching ability is to juggle two balls in one hand. Begin with one ball resting between your fingertips and the other in your palm. Throw the lead ball in a circle toward your body. When the first ball reaches the peak of the arc, toss the second ball in the air, catch the first, and so on. Once you master the technique, try moving the balls in a circle away from you, or tossing them straight up in parallel paths.

WALL JUGGLE

Using the two ball technique, stand three feet from a wall and toss your lead ball underhand about head-high against it. As it strikes the wall, toss the second ball, then catch the first. Continue juggling the balls like this while standing still, or while moving along the wall. After mastering this exercise, apply the same principles and juggle three balls using both hands. The system is the same as you learned earlier, except that the path of the ball is different.

JUGGLING CATCH

Face a teammate approximately eight feet away. At the beginning you hold two tennis balls, one in each hand, while your partner holds one ball in either hand. Toss one ball to your partner, who then tosses one ball back to you. Continue throwing and catching balls—this gets harder the faster you toss.

To make this drill more interesting, play a game up to 10—receiving a point when your opponent drops a ball. If two balls collide in the middle and you catch one on the rebound, you receive a point. After each point, the player who began with only one ball the previous time should begin with two balls. Move closer together, then farther apart, consistently challenging your opponent to time his catches and throws.

JUGGLING SNAG

Face a teammate approximately three feet away as he juggles three tennis balls. After ten seconds of juggling, snag one of his tennis balls as it hits its peak in the arc. Your partner should throw his next ball as if nothing had changed and you should also grab this one at its peak with your free hand. Now you have two balls, while he tosses his third and final ball. As this ball hits its peak, toss the ball in your right hand and snag the final ball, initiating the three ball juggle technique for yourself.

The switching from your partner's juggling to your juggling should be smooth and without pause. After you juggle for ten seconds, your partner should snag your tennis balls as you did his. This exchange should carry on until someone drops a ball or messes up an exchange.

WALL BALL

Holding two balls, stand five feet behind a teammate who is facing a wall. He should be crouched in his playing stance approximately one body length away from the wall. Throw a ball (overhand) over one of his shoulders. As the ball returns off the wall, his job is to catch it with either hand, as if he were catching a puck from a shooter. He should drop the balls behind him so you can pick them up for the next two throws. Continue throwing balls over both his shoulders, increasing velocity as his ability to catch improves.

WHERE THERE'S A WILL . . .

Although it would be nice if all athletes had state-of-the-art training facilities, such is not the case. This section has demonstrated many ways you can improve physically without relying on high-priced equipment and personal trainers. If you want something badly enough and are willing to work, there is always a way!

4

Setting Up to Make the Save

FIVE GOALTENDING KEYS

Five important points are as follows:

1. **Always square the hips and shoulders to the puck.** To give yourself the best opportunity to stop the puck, you must use your body's largest possible profile to cover the maximum amount of net. No matter where the puck is in its flight to the net, make sure you are square to it at all times.

Figure 4.1 There is no chance of the rebound going out in front on this save.

2. **Keep your hands up and out.** Many times you will see a goaltender drop his gloves to a lower position as he goes down into a save. This is a natural reaction, especially common among young goalies—as soon as they hit their knees, they drop their hands alongside their pads.

Be conscious of this tendency as you practice; if you get beat high after you went down into a save, ask yourself if your hands were too low—and, if so, determine whether it caused you to get beat. Ask yourself if perhaps you should have stayed on your feet.

Figure 4.2 Tom keeps his hands up as he drops into the butterfly, taking away both lower and upper parts of the net.

3. **Chest goes at the puck.** In analyzing saves, ask whether your chest moved toward the puck or away from it. One trick is to pay close attention to the symbol on your jersey—is it moving away from the puck while you're making a save? If so, it means you're pulling out, possibly afraid of the puck; it also can lead to your ending

Figure 4.3 Notice how the head, chest, and hips have all rotated to follow the puck, and the eyes follow the biscuit into the glove.

up on your back as the rebound lies in front of you. Your movement should be toward the object you are trying to stop, not away from it, but be careful to remain in control and not to lunge at the puck.

Get your chest and body moving at the puck and you will be right on top of the rebound, ready for a second or third shot, and able to quickly spring back onto your feet again. If the puck is heading for a certain area of the net, move as much of your body toward that area as possible.

4. **Watch the puck throughout the save.** You stop many pucks only at the very last moment. Crazy things can happen along a puck's path, such as dips or deflections. Watch the puck right into your equipment

Figure 4.4   Because the flight of the puck may change on the way to the net, you must watch it all the way in. Concentrate until the whistle has blown.

and trap it; or follow its direction after you have blocked it. If you lose sight of the puck, it can be in your net before you pick it up again. Your head and eyes tend to follow your chest. So if your chest is moving toward the puck, your eyes will have an easy time following its path.

5. **Keep your stick down.** Many goaltenders have a habit of picking up their sticks as they follow the play, so that quick low shot may sneak under the stick and into the net. If the stick isn't on the ice or on the floor, your chest will likely be too high—which means your balance will be off. In his book *Fuhr on Goaltending*, Grant Fuhr wrote that he places a bit of pressure on his stick to ensure the stick is on the ice.

Figure 4.5 A fundamentally sound goaltender always shows good form while moving from spot to spot.

THE STANCE

The stance is your foundation for success between the pipes. In today's game of lightning-fast shots, curved sticks, and big bodies blocking your vision, the quality of your stance is vital. You cannot afford to rely solely on reflexes.

A quality stance begins from the feet up. There are three important things to keep in mind for your stance:

- You must be solid on your skates to be able to react with correct form and to hold your position in traffic.
- Distribute your weight on the balls of your feet. Too much weight on your toes or heels leaves you in poor balance, diminishing your ability to perform saves and control rebounds.
- Bend your knees so that you sit comfortably and with confidence.

Figure 4.6   A solid stance is an essential building block for all goaltenders.

A proper stance is much like sitting on a horse. But when I work with younger goalies, I tell them to pretend they're sitting on a toilet—they tend to remember that one!

coaches' tip

It's imperative that you are comfortable in your stance while at the same time in the best position to react quickly to action.

The Triangle

Years ago they used to tell goalies to stand with their legs together. Today, goalies play with a triangular opening between their legs, allowing them to go down faster and cover the low corners better than with the standing style. Of course this leaves an opening at the five-hole, but it is a calculated risk. In in-line hockey, the lighter puck allows players to shelf it rather easily. So you should stay up as much as possible!

I believe the benefits of covering the low corners better and facilitating the butterfly move outweigh covering the five-hole, even though a goal scored between the legs is still misinterpreted as an easy one. Ninety-five percent of all shots are to the left or right of a goalkeeper's center point; whether they are high or low, he must react with lightning quickness. On those rare occasions when the puck is heading directly down the pipe, the goalie must reverse her outward movement and pull her body inward.

Knee Position

Many goalies have a bad habit in the way they position their knees. With the triangular stance, the pads meet at the knees. Some goalies press their knees together to create support for their bodies, so that it is the structure and not the thigh muscles (quadriceps) that support the weight of the body. This makes it less tiring for the goaltender to complete drills, but it also slows his reaction time and severely slows muscular development. The feet become like suction cups on the ice, and the goalie is trapped by his own stance. To react to a shot, the goalie must first come out of his position by popping up from that "knees-together" stance, and then go into the save—making two movements instead of one.

coaches' tip You may observe an improper knee position when a goaltender is tired and unconsciously taking pressure off his thighs. A telltale sign occurs in practice, when low shots are consistently being scored along the ice and the goalie's skates appear to be glued to the ice. He will appear knock-kneed as the puck enters the net.

Glove Position

Glove positioning is important in covering as much net as possible and in maintaining proper balance. Be sure that the blocker and catcher are at the same height, or parallel to each other. If one is higher than the other, an uneven distribution of weight will occur. For example, if your blocker is held high and your glove is low, more weight will be distributed on your glove side foot. Your goal is equal weight on both feet, to allow for quick reaction to either side. Keep your gloves forward and free to move in any direction.

Figure 4.7   Keep those gloves out and away from your body, so they are free to move in any direction.

There are two reasons why you must not hold your glove too high.

- Goalies can move the glove more quickly upward to catch a shot than downward.
- The puck rises from ice level, not waist level. Given the natural trajectory of the shot, you have a better probability of blocking it with your trapper at a lower position.

Many goalies employ two stances: one as they are setting up for the shot, the other at the moment the shot is released. By holding the glove higher in your initial stance, you can visually take away more net from the shooter. As he is shooting, lower the glove to be in line with the trajectory of the shot, which of course originates from ground level. Playing bigger early (rather than too compact) may give you a perceived advantage.

Many coaches spend too much time working on a goaltender's pre-stance, not realizing that when the shot is actually about to be released the goalie probably is in perfect symmetry. Unfortunately, the opposite is also often true: many goalies have a great stance right up until the release of the shot, but then they radically change their form. These goalies would benefit greatly from instruction and from use of videotape to help them see actions of which they're probably unaware.

Goaltenders should not hold their gloves directly at their sides. Move your hands forward, as if asking for the puck. Any inward movement of the gloves will be hampered by the pads and will cause a slight delay; or it may "handcuff" you from moving your gloves into position to make the save.

Try not to overlap the gloves with your pads. You want to cover as much net as possible. The catching glove must remain open. Make sure that the glove and blocker are fully facing the shot.

Posture and Stick

Your chest and shoulders must be squared to the puck, not the opposing player. Your chest should stick out in a convex position (imagine a rooster). You should be able to draw a straight line from the chest down to the pads. Make sure that your shoulders don't droop, as such a position can decrease coverage of the net an extra inch or two.

Hold the stick firmly, with a little pressure to the ice. The blade should lie between the legs 8 to 16 inches in front of the skates. This cushions the shot and minimizes the rebound. It also leaves the stick free to make a quick movement in the path of an arc.

Hold your head high, always facing toward the play. If it is difficult or tiring to hold your head back, it is probably because your shoulders are hunched over. From head to toe, your body should be in perfect symmetry and balance. A goaltender must be able to explode out of her stance and recover with sound mechanics. She must cover as much of the net as possible, while at the same time remaining compact enough not to show many holes.

HIP ROTATION

Your chest should always be oriented toward the puck. You can do this only if you rotate your hips while your upper torso moves in the appropriate direction. Many goaltenders lock their hips, so even though they execute the correct move, their bodies are not in position to cover as much of the net as they could otherwise. You want to move toward the puck (your upper body pointing toward it); but at the same time you should keep your lower body parallel with the opening of the net in order to maximize the area covered.

When the puck is in your zone, you adjust your position through lateral movement. But before you begin your stride to move right or left, rotate your hips *in the opposite direction* so that when you arrive at your destination you are already square to the puck. If the puck moves left, rotate your hips to the right, and vice versa. An obvious benefit is that if you don't arrive at that spot in time, you already have the biggest part of your body moving squarely toward the shot. Often you see goalies shuffle to an area and then square with the puck—but if they are too slow, they will have difficulty making the save.

If you have trouble with this move, imagine that you are executing a T-glide to the left. When you point your left toe out, what happens?

Figure 4.8   Tom is reading for the pass but is still playing the shot first, at this point.

Your hips rotate right as if they are on a swivel. You are now square to the spot you are moving to. Now move to that same spot with a power shuffle, but rotate your hips *before* you explode with your right leg.

Try to make a split save with your right skate and keep your hips from rotating. It won't happen. If you are facing a shot going top shelf to your glove side, your chest should go at the puck as you catch it. To do this properly, your hips must rotate to follow the puck into your glove. Since you want to be square to the puck whenever you can, you must rotate the hips in the opposite direction while moving to your right or left as shown below.

Figure 4.9 When moving, first rotate your hips, then follow the path of the puck while squaring off.

THE BASIC SAVES

You should master all of the following techniques. Practice them until you perform all the correct moves instinctively. It's a good idea to videotape yourself using each approach, then to compare what you see with the techniques described here. It's a gradual process, but well worth the effort.

The Butterfly

Traditionally, the stand-up style has been preferred to the butterfly. Attitudes are changing, however, and today a good butterfly is an excellent move to have in your repertoire. Many goaltenders rely heavily on this move; it is their recovery skills as much as their fundamentals that makes it effective. When going down into the butterfly position,

- leave your stick flat on the ice surface, covering the five-hole;
- spread your pads as far out as possible, covering the low corners;
- be sure you do not drop your gloves down to your knees as you descend; and
- hold your chest, shoulders, and head high, facing the puck.

BUTTERFLY—BASIC FORM

From the proper stance, drop to both knees, resting your weight primarily on the inner section of the knee. Spreading the pads in a "V" shape, cover the low corners and hold the gloves up and out in case

Figure 4.10   Don't lean back! Keep your chest up and over the puck.

of a high shot or deflection. When used correctly, the butterfly allows you to take away the low shot and to concentrate on moving your hands and stick.

As you drop to your knees, be conscious of the bend in your hips. Too much flexion in this area means the body will descend like an accordion, minimizing the amount of net the upper body will cover. There must always be some bend in the hips, or you will not be able to rotate and explode into another movement; but the higher the trajectory the puck must take to get in over your shoulder, the harder it is for the shooter to beat you. Try to keep your elbows in when you go down, blocking the shot that may otherwise pass under your armpits.

Keep your chest and shoulders high and over the puck. If you lean too far back, you will show more of the net than you should; you'll also be off balance, which won't let you react quickly to a shift in the play. If you lean too far forward, you may be able to cover the top of the net, but you'll be susceptible to a deke.

Commit to an all-or-nothing approach if you decide to use the butterfly. If you hesitate in your descent to the ice, you'll pay the price. Insecure goaltenders often fail to fully commit when going down; consequently, they give up weak goals. Don't get caught half way. Go down or stay up!

BUTTERFLY—RECOVERY

What really hurts a goaltender is not that she goes down too much— it's that she is too slow to get back on her feet. Goalies often neglect this skill in practice sessions, when there usually is time for them to recover at their own speed before preparing for the next shot. Always practice the quickest possible recovery from saves. It should become a reflex for you to pop up from a save.

Most young goaltenders learn to recover from the butterfly one leg at a time. If this is your approach, pick up your glove hand leg first. Don't drop your gloves when returning to your stance—keep them up and out, ready for a shot. Don't use them for support against your knees. Always keep your stick on the ice and covering the five-hole.

The quickest recovery from the butterfly is to spring up, both legs at the same time. This is sometimes difficult to learn, but constant practice will make it second nature. From the butterfly, exaggerate your crouch like an accordion contracting; rock slightly backward; and explode upward by contracting your thighs and pulling in your feet. At all times keep your gloves up and your stick on the ice.

Resume the proper stance. To learn the skill and increase speed, you can practice in full gear on the rubber flooring usually used in locker rooms and areas leading to the ice surface.

The Half Butterfly

The principles that apply to the butterfly also pertain to the half butterfly. In this move, the goaltender kicks out one leg instead of two. If the puck is shot along the ice, the pad should be left flat behind the stick blade. Be sure to angle the puck to the corner with the blade of your stick. If the puck is shot a foot or two off the ice, place the pad in a higher position with the stick remaining on the ice.

When you perform this move, be sure you have a bend in your knee. With a straight knee, your pad will be exactly square to the shooter—causing the rebound to go straight out and back into dangerous position. A bent knee will allow you to direct pucks to the corner and out of harm's way.

Hip rotation is extremely important in the half butterfly. As with the butterfly, rotate the hips opposite the direction in which the puck

Figure 4.11 By keeping a bend in the hip area and a bend in the knee, you can push pucks to the corner.

Figure 4.12   When executing this save, place your left foot slightly back behind your body so you can better control rebounds.

Figure 4.13   The first thing you must do is rotate your hips so that you move into the shot appearing as big as possible.

is headed: rotate to the right if the puck is to your left, and vice versa. This allows your torso to pivot while your chest goes toward and then over the puck. If you don't rotate your hips, you will be unable to follow the complete path of the puck and are likely to be left with a rebound that you are not in position to stop.

The Kick Save

Most goalies use the triangle stance and the butterfly, but haven't mastered the ability to turn the feet out on a kick save. If you kick out without turning the toe, your pad will face straight at the shooter. This tactic requires less timing and skill, and unfortunately, it leaves more rebounds. Turning the foot out will allow you to steer the rebound away from danger. You should use this technique when there is no chance of a screen, tip, or deflection. In traffic use a half butterfly or a skating butterfly, protecting the largest possible area of the net while performing the save.

Start by placing your right knee on the ice. With your left skate make a semicircle on the ice. Once you are comfortable, place your

Figure 4.14 The stick needs to cover the five-hole in case of a deflection or tip.

glove hand in position and follow your skate, with your stick ready to cover the five hole. Notice the movement of the pad, and anticipate where the rebound will end up once the save is made. Remember the rule, "Chest goes at the puck"; so don't pull away with your upper body as you kick out. Repeat the same procedure, but this time setting up on the left knee. Remember to play big by not bending forward too much or falling away.

coaches' tip   A goaltender should sometimes make an exaggerated kick save on a slow shot, whose speed increases the possibility of a bad rebound. To avoid leaving a juicy rebound for an opponent, the goalie kicks the puck using the stick and skate in a powerful explosion, sending the puck quickly away from the goal area. Although this creates a big rebound, it pushes the puck away from the attackers in front of the net.

The Shaft-Down Technique

The shaft down is the subject of much discussion among goalie coaches. Some feel it is a cop-out from playing a shot honestly, because there are obvious weaknesses and difficulty in controlling the rebound. But NHL goalies have shown the shaft down to be a useful tool. There is definitely a place for it, but more at some times than at others.

A good rule of thumb is that the closer the shooter, the more effective the shaft-down technique will be. If a player is cutting from one side of the ice to the other and you drop down early, you will not be able to follow him across the crease. If the shooter is approaching at a low angle, your best bet is still to play him square and on your feet.

On your right knee in the half butterfly, place your stick with the paddle flat along the ice. The blocker is effective in closing up the five-hole, and the stick should prevent any shots from going in along the ice. The key to a successful shaft-down technique is keeping your chest and shoulders up over the puck and your glove up and out.

The big liability, of course, is the high shot—especially to the blocker side. The closer the player is to you, the lower the risk,

EDDIE BELFOUR

In the '80s hockey coaches stressed to shooters that the best way to beat a goaltender was to keep the puck low and on the ice, and they were right. No wonder that in the '90s goalies have made a conscious effort to take away the low shot, forcing players to put the puck high. One of the first goaltenders to make use of the shaft-down technique is Eddie Belfour of the Dallas Stars. When Belfour broke into the NHL in the 1990-91 season he won both the Calder Trophy as the NHL's best rookie and the Vezina Trophy as the league's top goaltender. A big reason for Belfour's success is that he drastically limits the possibilities of allowing a goal against the lower portion of the net. He uses the shaft-down technique aggressively. This means he extends his stick and gloves forward to cut down the chance that a shot going high will get over him — playing the odds that he will either get a piece of the puck or that it will soar over the net.

© Picture Desk/Robert Skeoch

Figure 4.15   As with the butterfly, your percentages of stopping the puck with the shaft-down technique increase if you keep your chest up.

assuming you play big and square to the puck. Shaft down is also effective in a screen situation; many goaltenders prefer going down this way rather than with the butterfly. The shaft-down technique is extremely valuable when the goalie has to make a quick save to his glove side (possibly in a breakaway situation or goal mouth pass). Goaltenders often have used the two pad stack in this situation, but the shaft-down technique permits you to react more quickly and cover the ice better. Note that you are vulnerable when you use this technique on a screen shot from the point: you may see the puck at the last moment, but have your hands so low that you are unable to react quickly enough (although you will be in great shape if the shot is along the ice).

The Glove Save

Perhaps the most spectacular save for a goaltender is the big glove save. It is a great feeling when all parts of your body move in symmetry and culminate in a stoppage of play where the crowd can

Figure 4.16 Brett makes a glove save without opening up. This is a great idea, especially when there is traffic in front.

show its appreciation. The ability to catch the puck is essential to the success of a goaltender. A quick glove hand is not merely an advantage to your game—it is essential.

Being able to catch the puck cleanly lets you stop the game, thus giving you more control. It also means you will give up fewer rebounds and chances for your opponents. Make a conscious effort in practice to catch the puck at every opportunity. Whether the shot is coming at the top of your pads or your head, train your glove to snag pucks whenever possible. It will be hard at first; but if you can improve on this skill, your proficiency as a goaltender will dramatically increase.

GLOVE SAVE—BASIC FORM

Catching a puck is similar to catching a baseball. You want the puck to end up in your webbing. It will stick there and not bounce out as it would if you tried to catch it in the palm. It is important that you *watch* the puck go into your glove. If you don't watch the puck, that long slap shot that dips is going to make you look bad. As discussed in the stance section, be sure your glove is out and open. Don't handcuff yourself and don't hold your glove too high: you can move your glove up more quickly than you can bring it down.

Watch how a shortstop handles a grounder. He positions himself with his glove out and ready. As the ball is almost in his glove, he pulls his arms back to cushion the impact. Hockey players use this same technique as they take a pass—they control the puck and soften the contact by moving their stick with the puck. The same fundamentals apply to glove saves. Cushion the impact by moving with the puck rather than against it.

The glove save is performed standing up or going down in any number of the save techniques. Although the most exciting is the split glove save, try to use the half butterfly if you think the puck might be deflected.

GLOVE SAVE—CAVEATS

Many goaltenders use the glove save to express their acting ability. A great save is a boost to the team and takes the life away from an opponent; but too much exaggeration will make you look foolish and diminish the value of the stop. Give it some polish, but avoid theatrics.

Some goalies like to hold their glove out in the air after the stop, to get a whistle and show the world they caught it. A safer strategy, however, is to pull the glove into your body after the stop to protect both the puck and the health of your hand. Players may take a swing at the puck if they believe they can knock it free! And if you do drop the biscuit, it will be in front of the largest part of your body and not off to the side in front of an empty net.

The Blocker Save

The skill of using the blocker effectively is often taken for granted. Most goaltenders are able to use their blocker well enough, but someone who can manipulate the puck and control the play using blocker saves is noticeable. You can either steer the puck (normally to the corner) or trap the puck between the trapper and the blocker.

A shot stopped by the blocker should always be controlled. Angle the blocker in the direction you want the rebound to go. The puck will ricochet off the blocker and out of danger. Most of the time you will be angling the puck to the stick hand corner, but not always. If the shot comes from a tight angle on your glove side, you should be able to turn your blocker inward, thus directing the puck behind the goal

Figure 4.17 Tilt your blocker down to control rebounds.

Figure 4.18 Having the skill and confidence to catch pucks on your blocker will pay huge dividends.

Figure 4.19   Don't leave a careless rebound in the slot; steer it out of harm's way or freeze it.

line to your glove side. In this situation, a dangerous rebound may occur if you leave your blocker angling straight or outward. This move will be successful only if you hold your blocker in the proper position from the very beginning.

To control the puck better, tilt the blocker down as you direct the rebound into the corner. By not allowing the puck to fly into the glass, you decrease the possibility of unpredictable bounces.

The importance of being able to trap a puck between the blocker and glove cannot be overemphasized. Allow a shot to hit your blocker first, and then use the trapper to smother it. This technique requires great timing that comes only from constant repetition in practice. Be sure to follow the puck all the way, not allowing it to slip down to the ice. Don't use this trap technique only in ideal situations; practice trapping low and high shots, and trap pucks from the butterfly and half butterfly positions. With proficiency in this skill you can stop the play on most high shots, whether to your left or right.

The Two Pad Stack

The two pad stack is a valuable save because it can get your two biggest pieces of equipment over to cover unprotected net. The move requires timing and precise fundamentals.

A Note for In-Line Goalies

goalies' tip

This save is relevant mainly for ice players, as in-line goalies can't slide on the floor as can their counterparts on ice. You must be able to cover lateral passes, even though you are unable to shuffle or slide laterally as on ice. Stacking your pads on a lateral pass is very difficult for an in-line goalie.

TWO PAD STACK—GLOVE SIDE

Begin in your correct stance, then set your feet as if you are going to T-glide to that same side. After the push with your blocker side leg, throw that leg under your body and along the ice as your body moves in that direction. Stack the pads one on top of the other, forming a

Figure 4.20   Without using the stick to direct traffic, you are asking for trouble.

wall, and lay the side of your upper torso along the ice. Your glove should remain open and over your pads, while your blocker arm and stick point straight out. Make sure your armpit is in full contact with the ice, as this is a vulnerable area. Lay the stick out in front, to prevent the shooter from cutting to the middle of the net and leaving you stranded. If the attacker shoots into your body, quickly bring your stick in and your glove down to smother any possible rebound.

goalies' tip
The reason you leave your stick out is so the attacking player can't cut through the middle or pass the puck. When you know he's going to shoot, you can lay your stick down to cover the ice as you slide over to your glove side. For most situations I wouldn't recommend this technique, but if you know the tendencies of the shooter it can be very effective.

TWO PAD STACK—BLOCKER SIDE

Begin in your correct stance, then set your feet as if you are going to T-glide to the same side. After the push with your glove side leg, throw that leg under your body and along the ice as your body moves in that direction. Stack the pads one on top of the other, forming a wall, and lie on the side of your upper torso. Your blocker and stick should lie on top of the pads and should face the shooter. Stretch out your glove arm, to prevent the forward from cutting to the middle and to quickly smother rebounds. Remember to keep your armpit in contact with the ice.

TWO PAD STACK—TIPS

Don't allow yourself to fall back during execution of this stop. If your pads are tilted back, the shooter will have a better trajectory to lift the puck over you. A common problem is too much or too little bend in your waist when you're down on the ice. With too much bend, too much area is left uncovered; insufficient bend delays reaction time and recovery.

As in all saves, it is important to keep your eye on the puck. You can also use your head in this save to remind yourself to cover the hole underneath your armpit. As you hit the ice, lay your head, still

Figure 4.21 Extending the glove arm prevents a pass through the middle, and is useful for covering up rebounds.

watching the puck, on your shoulder. This should force your armpit onto the ice.

TWO PAD STACK—RECOVERY

Correct form in recovering from the two pad stack enables you to get up quickly and maintain the most advantageous position throughout the procedure. The goal is that, during each step of the recovery, you are in position to cover as much net as possible and to react to a shot.

RECOVERY—Glove Side: When recovering from a stack to the glove side, first bend your bottom leg to a 90-degree angle. Pull your blocker hand inward and push your weight off the ice until you are on that one knee. You should be in a half butterfly position, with your glove out and open and your stick on the ice covering the five-hole. Now push yourself up with the power generated from the bent leg, using the stability of the glove hand skate.

Remember to always stay square, facing the puck with your head, shoulders, and hips. As your skill increases, your recovery should become more fluid. Young goaltenders may have trouble with this move because of a lack of strength in their arms.

a

b

Figure 4.22 (a) Proper form in the stack; (b) only use one hand in pushing up.

c

d

Figure 4.22 *(continued)* (c) proceed into a half butterfly; (d) resume the stance.

RECOVERY—Blocker Side: Recovering from a stack to the blocker side is similar to recovery to the glove side. Bend your bottom leg to a 90-degree angle. Pull your glove hand inward, and push your weight off the ice until you are on that one knee. You should be in a half butterfly position, with your blocker up and out and your stick on the ice covering the five-hole. Now push yourself up with the power generated from the bent leg and using the stability of the blocker hand skate.

Always stay square, facing the puck with your head, shoulders, and hips. You'll know you've mastered this technique when placing weight on your bottom knee is no longer necessary and you can get up in one fluid motion rather than in steps.

Stick Save

Sometimes a puck will come at such a great speed or from such close range that it is impossible to move your body as you would like. Without leaving your feet, you can redirect a quick shot along the ice into the corner with just a short pass with the stick. You should be able to move your blade along an arc in front of the pads.

Practice this save with a shooter in the slot firing pucks left and right of you. After having him slow down the velocity a notch, practice the same stick movements performing butterfly and half butterfly saves.

Figure 4.23 By keeping your hands out in front of your body, you are free to move the stick in a semicircular motion to stop a quick shot.

The Poke Check

One of the most lethal weapons in a goaltender's arsenal is the poke check. As effective as it can be, if executed incorrectly it can spell trouble. There are different techniques and strategies connected with the poke check.

There are two ways to shoot your stick out in this move.

- You can propel the stick by pushing out at the top of the paddle. As the stick slides forward, the shaft of the stick will glide through your hand. Just as you approach impact, catch the stick at its knob. This approach is best used to camouflage the ensuing poke check.

a

b

Figure 4.24 (a) Brett slides his hand up the shaft to grab the knob and poke check with power; (b) by letting the shaft slide as you poke, you can surprise the shooter.

- Slide your hand up the shaft of the stick and grab firmly at the knob. Propel the stick toward the puck with control. Although this approach allows you to throw your stick out with power and confidence, it may tip off the shooter.

Figure 4.25   If you're going to poke check, make it all or nothing.

BLOCKER SIDE POKE CHECK

From a stopped position, generate forward momentum by turning your blocker side foot out in an open T-glide position. Bend at the knees and waist, exploding at the puck while staying low. Propel the stick forward using one of the techniques discussed above. Land on the ice with your body extended and your head up following the course of the puck.

Key to a successful poke are the elements of surprise and timing. If an opponent has her head up she will see the poke coming and walk around you. Try to catch the shooter with her head down. Time your poke so that the blade thrusts through the interception point. If you throw it too early, the player will walk around you and tuck the puck into the empty net.

The wider the angle that the forward is cutting to the net, the better chance you have to take the puck. If you try to poke check a player coming down the pipe, he can easily maneuver left or right, giving him a high probability of beating the move. If the shooter is sweeping in at an angle, his momentum is set and he will have a hard time adjusting his path—thus giving the goaltender the advantage.

GLOVE SIDE POKE CHECK

There are two ways to poke check players approaching from the glove side.

- From a stopped position, execute a two pad stack starting in the T-glide position. The stick should be facing toward the center of the ice; the glove should be over the pad, ready to react if a quick shot is released. Unlike with a poke check to the blocker side, when going to the glove side you should leave the stick along the ice to block the path of the puck rather than to intercept it at a particular point. This move is successful most often when the player is cutting toward the middle of the net on his off wing (backhand). Your ability to execute this tactic will require timing and a lot of practice. As with the poke check from the blocker side, don't become predictable by using the poke too often—otherwise your opponents will be prepared, eliminating the element of surprise.

- From a stopped position, drop your blocker side knee toward the ice and bend at the waist. Turn the blade of your stick to an outward

Figure 4.26 This save demands a lot of practice and timing, but can be quite effective.

Figure 4.27   Any time you can stop a pass from heading to a high percentage scoring area, you have saved yourself some trouble.

position and thrust your stick at the puck while keeping your head up. The optimum time to use this technique is when the player is trying to walk out from the corner, close to the net. As he crosses over the goal line, you can surprise him and poke the puck away as he searches for a player to dish the puck off to.

POKE CHECK—TIPS

Poke check situations are dictated by the path of the player, the position of the defense, and your opponent's distance from the net. But you can also set a player up for the poke check, much like you can entice a player to shoot where you want as discussed in the breakaway section in chapter 6.

When a player is cutting to the net from an angle, he expects you to follow him across the crease and backward to make the save. When this occurs, you can implement a technique I call *standing up the shooter*.

When the forward is bearing down on the net, watching the puck, *abruptly stop your backward motion and hold your ground*. By the time he picks his head up again he will be very close to you and confused: the last time he saw you, you were skating backward, and he projected you to be deeper in the net. At this point you can poke check him; or if he is right on top of you, you can use the half poke.

a

b

c

Figure 4.28 (a) Tom comes out to challenge; (b) he C-cuts backward to the top of the crease; (c) a half poke may be all he needs.

The Half Poke

You can use the half poke from either side. Intercept the puck by staying on your feet and poking, generating the power from a firm grip on the paddle. In this move you do not slide your hand up the shaft of the stick—your goal is to quickly shoot the blade at the puck and remain on your feet so that you are prepared to follow the puck. Execute the exact same move when an opponent attacks on your glove side, except turn the blade over so that it is facing out instead of in.

a

b

Figure 4.29a-b A quick extension of the stick allows you to poke check but remain standing.

Set up drills in which your goaltenders can practice specific techniques such as standing up the shooter. Question them after the drills, to confirm that they understand their own weaknesses and strengths and to keep them conscious of how they read their opponents. They may find, for example, that many players are so unobservant that they will almost run into the goalie—and the majority of the time the goalkeeper can block the puck simply because of his position, with little need to do anything more than just stand there. It is important that your goalies understand the specific purpose of any given drill.

RECOVERY TECHNIQUES

Even the most dramatic saves are in vain if you can't get back into position as quickly as possible. Practice proper recovery technique as carefully as you practice saves, lest your other efforts be wasted in the end.

Recovery From Your Back

One of the most helpless feelings a goaltender can have is to be lying flat on his back staring at the lights. It is imperative to make a quick and smart recovery. This technique needs a lot of training, and younger goalies will have a tough go of it—but it will come in handy in the long run.

Your first job is to find the puck. Bend up from the waist so that your upper body is covering part of the net and your gloves can react to a shot. When the puck is in sight, put your stick in front of you and place your glove on the ice. Do not place your blocker on the ice—you should develop enough upper-body strength so that you only need to use one arm to get up. This leaves your other arm free to stop the puck.

Bend at your knees and push yourself up, straight ahead, with your stick on the ice at all times. Resume the proper stance as soon as possible.

You should resist rolling over, using two hands, or going to a butterfly, even if you're faster using these methods at first. Persevere in learning to get up the proper way. Remember to keep the puck in sight at all times, and try to keep your shoulders and hips square.

Recovery From Your Stomach

Being face down and flat on the ice is not the best position to stop a shot or rebound but this is sometimes the case. Recovery must be quick and intelligent.

Your first task, as always, is to get sight of the puck. With both hands on the ice, push yourself into the butterfly position. Quickly pull your hands up and into proper alignment. Get the blade of the stick flat on the ice, covering the five-hole. From the butterfly position, return to proper stance using the techniques as described under butterfly recovery.

KEEP PRACTICING!

Natural ability and good instincts are essential for a goaltender. Without learning basic form and constantly practicing fundamentals, however, you will never reach your full potential. Constant repetition and correction will help ingrain correct form into your muscle memory. This is why even pro goaltenders need goalie coaches and go to camps in the summertime, to refresh themselves on the fundamentals that got them where they are today.

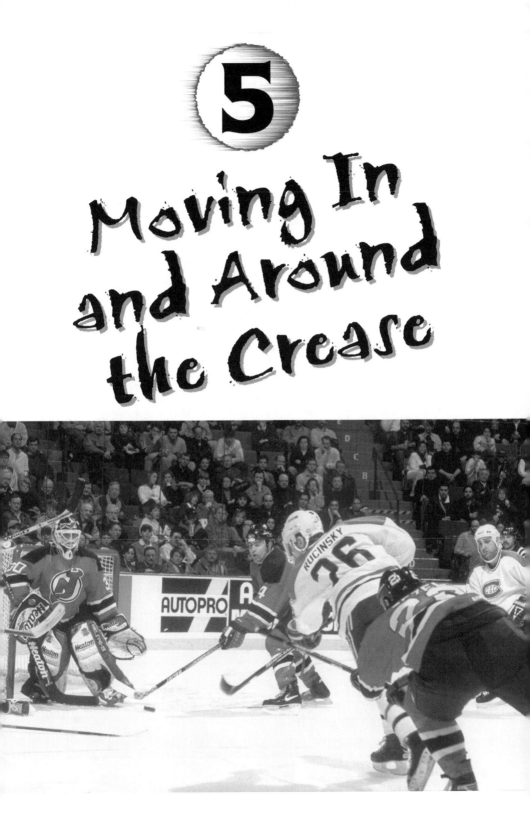

5

Moving In
and Around
the Crease

In today's game you must be able to move in and out of your crease area. The more quickly you can move from one spot to another, the greater your probability of stopping a shot. In this section we will go over the various ways a goaltender moves. Later, we'll explain how to put power into those movements.

STARTING POINT

Position yourself in the middle or peak of your semicircular crease. When the puck moves left or right on the other side of center ice, you should remain at the same spot. Resist the temptation of moving side to side.

The benefit of using this spot as a starting point is that when the play does come your way, only a minimal adjustment is necessary to get on your angle. You will not risk being caught too deep in your crease and susceptive to a long shot. If you pick a spot deep in your crease to begin with, as the play approaches you have to make large adjustments and may be caught deep in your net. Or, a pass may be made forcing you to make further adjustments before you have reached the initial spot you were moving to.

Figure 5.1   It's a great habit to always start from the same place.

SKATING

I highly recommend using videotape to check your progress in learning good skating techniques. It's difficult to analyze important subtleties in your movements while you're actually doing them. Read over this section several times, then practice each technique while videotaping your efforts; then analyze where you need to improve, and practice some more.

The C-Cut

Backward and forward movements are the result of a technique called the C-cut. To move forward, the goaltender (in his stance) propels himself by putting pressure on the heel of one of his feet while it is angled slightly to the outside. He then pushes his foot through the path of an arc and transfers his weight to the other foot at the same time. The skating motion should not affect the quality of the stance. The stick should remain on the ice; the hips, shoulders, and chest should face constantly forward; and the head should remain high, facing the puck.

The only significant body movement you should see is in the feet and pads. If the rest of the body is bobbing up and down, there is something wrong. The goalie should try to stop on her outside foot, or the foot closest to the play: that way if the puck moves to the opposite side of the ice, her weight is already on the proper foot.

If you read the play as a clear shooting situation, however, you may elect to stop on your inside foot or the foot furthest away from the play. By doing this you angle your hips and shoulder better than if you stopped on the outside foot, enabling you to steer the puck into the corner and decreasing the odds that the rebound will end up in front of the net and in a prime scoring area.

A similar motion is created when you move back toward the net, the only difference here being that you transfer your weight to the ball of the designated pushing foot to begin the C-cut or arc. Again, you should try to stop your momentum on the foot closest to the play.

With this skating maneuver there will obviously be a gap between your legs as you move back and forth. You should become proficient in using a *quick* C-cut—or a longer, more powerful one. Take smaller strides only when making slight adjustments in a shooting situation. Use a larger C-cut when you want to cover a maximum amount of area

Figure 5.2   A clear-cut shooting situation.

in the shortest amount of time. For example, when the puck is passed from the corner to the point man, you want to establish an aggressive position at the top of the crease. Work on both techniques: tight C-cuts for quickness, and larger C-cuts for power.

Moving Side to Side

There are two techniques in moving side to side—the shuffle and the T-glide.

THE SHUFFLE

The shuffle is most useful in making small adjustments in your positioning.

In your stance, push off on your inside edge to propel yourself left or right. Then transfer your weight to the opposite foot, which glides along the ice until it stops your sideways momentum. In-line goaltenders must pick up that lead foot as they generate power from the other skate.

When using the shuffle, work on keeping your stance steady and your body square to the puck. Keep the stick on the ice, your gloves level and out, your trapper open, and your head up. Sometimes younger goalies get into the bad habit of watching their feet or staring at the ice while doing drills involving skating. Make sure your head always follows the play. Once you have developed power in a shuffle, you'll be able to execute the post-to-post shuffle by a single power push.

Lay a stick across the goaltender's gloves and tell her to imagine a glass of water balancing in the middle of the stick. The water should not spill if the goaltender doesn't bob during each stride.

coaches' tip

Figure 5.3 Head up, shoulders square, stick on the ice, no bobbing, gloves open and out.

THE T-GLIDE

You can cover more lateral distance using a T-glide than you can with a shuffle.

This stride is executed by pointing your nonweightbearing foot at a 90-degree angle and pushing off the inside edge of the other skate. Glide to your desired position on the lead foot, and stop momentum by turning that foot back to its original position in the stance. Maintain your stance, remembering not to bob or take your stick off the ice throughout the entire movement.

A lot of goaltenders have trouble remaining square to the play when performing a T-glide. Pay close attention to your lead shoulder, as this is what usually throws the whole stance off. Make sure this shoulder is not pulled back, thereby throwing your hips off and moving your stick away from covering the five-hole.

Figure 5.4   You can cover a lot of ice quickly with the T-glide.

Younger goaltenders use the T-glide to get from post to post; an experienced goalie should use a single power shuffle. The T-glide is an effective tool when an opponent is in tight on the goal. If the opponent cuts in front of the goal mouth, it is very difficult to follow him across the crease with a series of shuffles—each shuffle could leave a juicy five-hole in which to shoot. Using the T-glide, you should be able to stay right on top of the shooter throughout his attack. After the initial push, you may want to limit the five-hole and far corner shot by dragging your back leg across the ice in tight with your lead leg. This position allows you cover the short side and explode into a kick save to the far side.

When executing this strategy, remember to keep your stick on the ice and your gloves up as shown below.

Figure 5.5   A leg drag can be an effective technique coming off of a T-glide.

Explosive Movement

When a goaltender changes his positioning, the speed with which he arrives at the next spot has a major impact on his ability to make the save. In practice sessions, there tends to be an unrealistic surplus of time for the goalie to "get over" and into position between shots.

The worst scenario for a goaltender is to be caught moving forward when the shot is being released. That is why goalies are always taught to stop on the shot. The more quickly the goaltender moves to challenge a shooter, the farther out he will get and the more time he will have to stop and set himself.

Concentrate on exploding from spot to spot. Eventually this will become a habit and will contribute to your success. If you have a few minutes during practice, set two pucks or gloves about six feet apart from each other. Staying in your stance, practice exploding from one glove to the other using the shuffle and the T-glide techniques. Challenge yourself by moving the gloves farther apart, and practice reaching your destination in one powerful stride.

Figure 5.6　Maintain proper form while working on increasing your range.

PATRICK ROY

Patrick Roy has long been considered one of the best goalies in the NHL. Most goaltenders would give their right arm to be blessed with his combination of size, strength, and athletic ability. So you would think that these talents would be the focal point of his style... Wrong — Roy is one of the many goaltenders in the '90s who realizes the importance of positioning and deemphasizes flashy acrobatic saves. "I'm not going to do the spectacular split saves or stack my pads sliding across the crease," he says. "If I'm not in proper position, I'm not going to make the save." Therefore Roy uses his experience to read the play, determine where the shot will be released, and position himself so that the least amount of net is showing for the shooter. This forces the shooter to make a great shot if he is going to beat Roy. Roy uses the butterfly save with exceptional effectiveness. In the butterfly, Roy spreads his pads out to cover the ice, keeps his chest up to block a high shot, and keeps his gloves up and out, forcing the trajectory of the shot to be very steep to beat him. He also keeps his elbows in rather than out in order to stop a shot that might otherwise go in underneath his armpits.

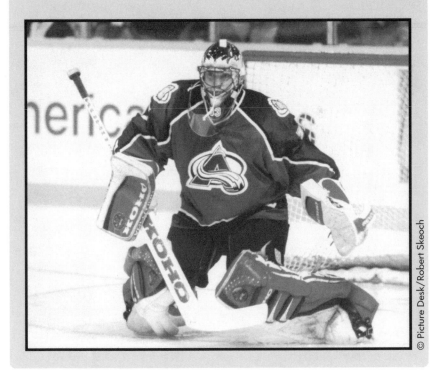

© Picture Desk/Robert Skeoch

MOVEMENT ALONG THE ARC

Ten years ago scouts and coaches believed lateral movement was the most essential element to a goaltender's success. Today, although lateral movement is necessary in post-to-post, behind-the-net coverage, goalies use more semicircular than direct left-right adjustments.

In figure 5.7, notice how the goalkeeper follows the shooter along an arc (in this case the crease), enabling the goalie to have better odds at stopping the puck throughout the path of the opponent. In figure 5.8, where the goalie challenges the shooter using lateral movement, notice how the opponent increases his scoring percentage by moving toward the center of the ice.

Some goaltenders have difficulty learning to follow the play along an imaginary arc, either because of their weak skating ability or because they have already formed bad habits. With hard and persistent practice, however, the movement can become as natural to you as walking. And once you incorporate into your game this ability to always give yourself the most advantageous position, the results will be dramatic.

Figure 5.7a-b Tom maintains his positioning while following the shooter.

Figure 5.8a-b   Brett does not maintain his positioning and ends up showing too much net.

PLAYING ANGLES

Flashy goaltenders who make a lot of acrobatic saves receive a lot of attention. But have you ever considered why they have to make so many exaggerated stops? Often it's because they are often caught showing too much of the net—and then they have to scramble dramatically to make the save! A goalie proficient in playing his angles makes the game simpler and reduces the probability of giving up a goal.

The easiest way to understand the importance of knowing your angles is to tie ropes to both posts, long enough so that a person can simulate the position of a shooter. Have your coach hold the ropes taut with one hand, and set up at various points (e.g., the most common shooting positions, somewhere between the face-off dots). As he does this, try to stay square to his position, and center yourself between the two ropes. When you're square to the puck and centered between the ropes, you're in the ideal spot. Try moving forward and backward to see how much more of the net you can cut off—if you're too deep there will be lots of room between you and the ropes. Extra space on one side is an open target for the shooter to put the puck past you. During a game, you can't see the net behind you while simultaneously keeping your eyes on the puck, so this drill teaches you how to cut off the angles and cover the net. Set up a practice session where your coach skates to several positions around the zone, and you have to follow while staying midway between the ropes. This will teach you how to position yourself instinctively when you challenge a shooter during a game.

Staying Perpendicular to the Puck

To take maximum advantage of her equipment's surface area in blocking the path of a shot, a goalie's head, shoulders, and pads should be square to (i.e., directly facing) the puck. As the puck moves, the goaltender continuously adjusts her position so she is square to the shot.

In the rope exercise, check to see if the tips of your skates always point directly at the coach as he moves around the crease (or at the puck, if your coach is equipped with a stick and puck). If they are, this means that both your hips and shoulders are square to the shooter (to the puck). This is perfect. Even if you are positioned correctly on the angle, you put yourself at a disadvantage by not being square with the puck.

Do the rope exercise while standing on the semicircular goal crease. When you believe you are on your angle and square to the shooter, look down to see where your skates cut through the goal crease. If your blades are running parallel to one another and perpendicular to the crease, this means your body is square to the puck, giving yourself the maximum advantage. You can use this check throughout practice sessions.

Goaltenders often err by squaring with the shooter rather than the puck. The shooter can deceive a goaltender by leaning in one direction while controlling the puck with her stick fully extended. Have the coach control the rope through the use of his stick. Notice the difference when you line up with the coach and when you line up with the puck.

Don't be shy about tapping the posts with your stick or glove to check your position. Knowing that you are on your angle will add to your confidence and therefore increase your effectiveness. Remember to stop on the outside foot when you are moving out on your angle. Take advantage of markings on the ice and on the boards that can confirm you are on the angle.

Figure 5.9 A great way to check your angles.

coaches' tip

Younger goalies tend always to be square to center ice; as the play moves right or left of the midline, they move their skates laterally but don't square up their bodies. Here's a good drill. The goalie begins in her stance with her stick laid out in front of her. With her gloves out in front of her body, she should step over the stick with her left leg, then step back with the same leg. Have her do the same with her right leg, continuously alternating both sides. To ensure that she is leading with her hands, have her pretend she is holding a steering wheel. This ensures that when she steps she has both hands in front—as if pushing the hypothetical puck toward the side where she is stepping.

Taking Away Zones

Positioning is critical in today's brand of hockey, where the skating is quick and shots come in hard and fast. Your best chance is to play the angles, which increases the odds you'll make the save. This is called "playing the percentages." When you clearly see the shot and have time to make the save, by all means do so. But what about (for example) a quick pass to your glove side, when the receiver of a pass is about to one-time the puck seven feet outside your crease? A save is out of the question. All you can do is take away as much of the net as possible and hope to block the puck.

In taking away a zone, it is essential that you square yourself fully to the direction the shot is coming from. Many goaltenders use the shaft-down technique, or butterflies or half butterflies. The idea is to cover the bottom of the net—and, by keeping your chest up, to force the shooter to pick one of the upper corners. If he hits the shot, he's

Figure 5.10   Not much of a chance for the shooter.

got you; but you're betting that the shooter will miss the net or that you will get a piece of it. A good goaltender will quickly drop into one of these saves during a goal mouth scramble or a wraparound, playing as big as possible.

Skating Saves

It is important that goaltenders practice skating saves. A skating save occurs when a goaltender moves from one area of the net (generally by a T-glide or shuffle) and covers another area of the net using a skating butterfly, half butterfly, or shaft-down technique. In these moves it is imperative that your shoulders stay square to the puck and that you move quickly. Skating saves allow you to drive into the puck and push the rebounds to the corners.

PROPER POSITIONING

It is dangerous for a goaltender to play deep in his net, relying solely on his reflexes and athletic ability rather than playing the percentages. Regardless of how confident you may be of your abilities, you can always improve your game by being positioned properly.

Proper positioning takes hard work and conditioning. When playing deep you don't have to move as much while following the puck; but if you want to station yourself for the best opportunity of making the save, a lot more movement is necessary.

It has already been pointed out that the best place to be as the play moves in your direction is at the top of your crease. You will need to make minimal lateral adjustment as players advance between center ice and the near blue line. To best cut down the angle, you should move beyond the crease. It is from this position that you can begin your backward motion as the puck moves deeper into the zone. But note: you don't want to move far out too early, or you may be stranded by a cross-ice pass or unable to stop a puck dumped in behind the net.

Consider the strategy discussed in the section on playing angles: the farther you move toward the shooter, the more you cut the angle.

Obviously you cannot neglect the risk taken by playing too aggressively—this is why you continually move forward and backward with the play. You invite trouble, however, when you begin to glide back and forth rather than explode into position. A telltale sign of a tired goaltender is that he picks his chest up when moving, neglecting to stay in his stance, and that he lifts his stick off the ice.

Figure 5.11   Why give the shooter a chance? Come out and take the net away.

6
Challenging the Shooter

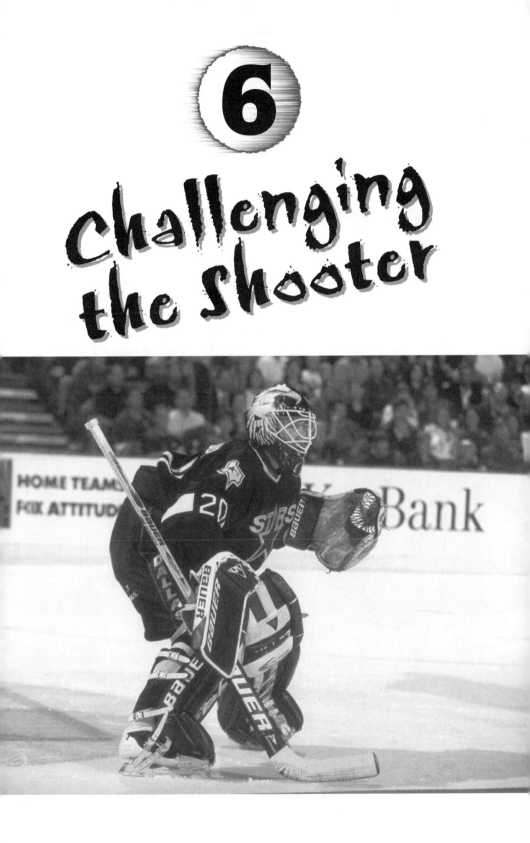

Talent can take you only so far. Without combining skill and intelligence, a goaltender will never reach his or her full potential. This manual offers alternative approaches to many situations; I encourage you to experiment, adapting new concepts and techniques in order to lift your level of play.

KNOW WHAT'S GOING ON

An intelligent goaltender can greatly help herself and her team by making smart decisions. The only way to make these correct decisions, however, is to always know the situation of the game as well as the personnel. Being able to freeze the puck gives you the power to control tempo, momentum, and line changes.

When a quarterback lines up to take a snapped football on a passing play, before he gets the ball he knows what all his players will be doing and what his options will be when he drops back to pass. This allows him to read the defense and make the right choices. Imagine what would happen if that quarterback didn't know what patterns his receivers would be running when he got the ball. The same rationale applies to the goaltender and his teammates in respect to how he will play certain situations. Be prepared!

You should always be aware of what's going on throughout the game. Continuously thinking will allow you to concentrate better and not have lulls when your mind starts to drift. Your head for the game will show your teammates and scouts that you are alert and ready.

coaches' tip	Here's a good tactic for helping your goalies become more mentally alert: after a goal is scored in a scrimmage, have your goalie give you a detailed verbal description of where everyone on the ice was when the goal was scored.

You should know which way each of your defensemen shoots. This will help you place the puck conveniently for them and aid in the breakout. For every action there is a reaction. If you and your

Below are a list of questions you should ask yourself when deciding whether to take a whistle or move the puck. Before you are even in the situation to move the puck, you should already know the answers to these questions:

goalies' tip

- How much traffic is around me, and what kind of risk will I take if I move the puck?

- Is one of my teammates clearly open to take a pass? What will my recovery options be if we lose possession of the puck?

- Are my teammates tired because they've been on for a long shift?

- If I freeze the puck, can it stop the other team's momentum and give us a chance to regroup—or, if my team has been forcing the play, will it slow our momentum?

- How much time is left in the period (you don't want to take any chances going into an intermission)?

- Has one of my teammates broken/lost a stick or edge?

- Is there a line mismatch? Do they have their best personnel on the ice while we have our worst?

- How strong is my ability to make the play? What are the percentages?

- Am I mentally or physically tired, needing a break?

- Will this control and stoppage lend me confidence?

teammates are prepared to handle the numerous situations that may exist within a game, chances are your reactions will come more quickly and be made with more confidence.

THE BREAKAWAY

The approach you take in handling a breakaway is very individual. There is no right or wrong strategy, but it should reflect your strengths.

Technique

After identifying the breakaway, position yourself in front of the crease in order to be capable of moving backward as the player approaches. You must be far enough out not to show too much of the net, but not so far as to allow the shooter an easy deke. Use C-cuts as you move backward with the player, trying not to give up an easy between-the-legs goal. Be ready at all times for a quick shot and have the ability to move right or left, making a save on the deke. A cardinal rule for the goaltender is *never to make the first move*; but a smart netminder can sometimes dictate the actions of the shooter just by his positioning and tactics.

I am often asked how far a goaltender should come out to meet the shooter. This depends on your skill in skating backward. If you can skate well, there is no reason to show the shooter a lot of the net to begin with. Challenge him, so that when he picks his head up he sees an opponent with confidence—this gives you the psychological advantage.

Figure 6.1 Timing is everything. Work to your strengths.

If you are coming out to face the shooter you are also challenging him to beat you with a deke. You are one step up on him, because just by your positioning you are coaxing him into your trap. If you are not a great skater, don't come out too far from the crease—the most important factor in this situation is timing.

Wherever you position yourself, anticipate the timing of your backward motion in accordance with the speed of your opponent's approach. Skate backward too fast and you end up too deep in your crease, showing the player too much mesh; if you're too slow, he will walk around you.

To learn exactly what your rhythm is, take a lot of breakaways in practice. *Don't let the players approach at half speed when you're doing drills*—this will hurt you in a game. Practice coming way out and playing shallow. If you are comfortable in practice, your confidence will lead to big saves during games. If you spend little time and thought on your approach during practice, a breakaway in a game will become a crisis rather than an exciting challenge.

Taking Charge

You can fool the shooter into doing what you want by showing him an opening to shoot for. Most good goalies are confident in their glove hand and may show a hole on the glove side to encourage the shooter to beat him there. This puts you at an advantage, because you know where the puck is going to go. When the player takes the bait and shoots for the hole, you pounce and snag the puck with the lightning quickness you've attained during practices. Experiment with this move in practice. Don't use it too frequently or you'll become predictable—instead, save it for when you feel you can trap the shooter.

Sometimes the goaltender makes the first move and poke checks the puck carrier. (See chapter 4 for discussion of the poke check technique.) Use this move in a breakaway situation only if you have the angle on the shooter and he is attacking on your stick hand side. Don't attempt the poke check if she is coming down the middle: the odds are too low in this situation, and if you miss you'll look very bad. If she comes from your glove side, poke check only if you have confidence in your ability to perform this difficult save.

Figure 6.2 One option is to show it and then take it away.

Dekes

There are no hard rules about which saves to use against a deke; you'll have to determine what works for you. I sometimes show goalies how to use the two pad stack, but this isn't always the best approach. The stack allows you to cover a lot of net, and the shooter has to make a great shot to get it over you—but if you're too slow in executing the stack, the shooter will slide the puck into an open cage.

The longer you can stay on your feet, the better. And if you're quicker and more confident stacking to your blocker side or using the shaft-down technique on your glove side, do what suits you best. Work hard in practice on your repertoire of moves. Repetition makes your moves quicker and allows you more options in a game situation. It should be your goal to practice each move until it is second nature to you.

PENALTY SHOTS

In ice hockey, you can do a couple of things to help yourself in a penalty shot situation. As soon as possible after the penalty shot has been called, sweep the snow that has built up on the side of the crease toward the slot area. This may make it difficult for the shooter to control the puck as he approaches the net. If you are heading into penalty shots at the conclusion of a tied game, sweep the snow out front right after you hear the siren and before you skate to the bench. The linesmen will clear the snow from the posts and check the netting only just before the shoot-out begins.

After a penalty shot has been called, concentrate on your breathing. The excitement could trigger you to breathe too fast, which will diminish your effectiveness. Slow down your breathing pattern by taking long deep breaths and exhaling slowly; this will improve your coordination and your poise. Next time you watch a basketball game, pay close attention to a player preparing to take a free throw. She has been running up and down the court so she must settle her nervous system down in order to have the poise to make the foul shot. She does this by controlling her breathing pattern.

Odd Man Breaks

The following situations require a great deal of coordinated practice between you and your defensemen. Practice until you act as a unit, each knowing precisely what his teammates are doing.

THE ONE-ON-ONE

A 1-on-1 situation isn't an odd man break, but it can quickly become a 1-on-0 break if the offensive player beats your defense. Very rarely should a goal be given up in a 1-on-1 situation. It is up to you to make sure the defense is clear on how you want this played.

The goal of the 1-on-1 situation is to give the shooter the worst possible angle in which to shoot. The defense should occupy the middle of the ice surface, putting the odds in your favor.

Gap control is an essential element to this strategy. If your opponent is angled to one side but given lots of room to take a big windup, her percentages are increased. If your defense stays close to the shooter, the shot will be rushed.

Don't let a lazy defenseman be used as a screen by your opponent. A player will take advantage of loose gap control and release her shot directly in front of your defenseman, hoping that you will lose track of the puck and not be able to read the release point. A defenseman who never gets beat in a 1-on-1 situation is probably not playing tight enough and is giving up scoring opportunities in other forms.

THE TWO-ON-ONE

The 2-on-1 requires confidence and communication between the goaltender and defensemen. The object is for the defenseman to take responsibility for the pass and the goaltender to play the shooter.

The defenseman tries to place himself between the open man and the puck carrier. He must try to stay in the middle of the ice surface, forcing the shooter to release on a bad angle. The goaltender challenges the shooter, trusting his teammate to intercept an attempted pass. The more the defenseman covers the open player and allows the puck carrier more room in the middle, the greater the disadvantage to the goalie.

Teams must spend time practicing the 2-on-1, so the defensemen can get to know their goaltenders. There is a big difference between how an aggressive goalie and a patient goalie will play this situation. When the aggressive goaltender identifies the shooter, she will immediately come out and challenge—which means that an early pass in the zone could trap her, leaving an empty net for the pass recipient. The defenseman must know in advance how his goalie will react. If he knows the goalie is aggressive, he will quickly take responsibility to cover the pass; if he knows his goalie is more patient and waits longer for plays to develop before challenging a shooter, he will take more time to force the shooter to a tougher angle.

Be aware of a common mistake made by defensemen close to the net in 2-on-1 situations: Once the defensemen get close to the crease, they often peel off to tie up their man. The problem comes when they peel off early, allowing the shooter the option of cutting in front of the net. The defenseman must stay in the middle all the way to the top of the crease, thus forcing the shooter to release at a tough angle and give the goalie a greater chance to make the stop. The shooter must not be given the option of cutting across the net to the far side—he must be cut off.

As a goalie, you must take the responsibility to explain to your teammates how you want the 2-on-1 played. Don't let your defense make the same mistakes over and over without being corrected. In the end, you are the one who looks bad.

THE TWO-ON-NONE

Facing two attackers can be an intimidating situation to a goaltender, but you are not without recourse. The most important point to remember is not to let one player isolate you, leaving an empty net

Figure 6.3 This is an aggressive move.

if the second player receives the pass. This is often a tough job for aggressive netminders who like to challenging the puck carrier.

When identifying the 2-on-0, resist the temptation to play too aggressively. Come out of your net and position yourself conservatively, ready to skate backward with the right timing as in the breakaway situation. The old rule remains intact: "Always play the shooter." But don't let her pull you so far away that you'll be unable to play the second opponent if she passes. Always be in position to react to the shot, deke, or pass.

Some goalies will try to take away the pass by using the stack and poke at the same time. This is okay when the shooter is at a bad angle, coming in on the goaltender's glove side. But if the two players are fairly close to each other and coming straight down the pipe, by all means stay on your feet; and if the players are drawn close enough inward, you can use a half poke check to intercept an attempted pass.

Another tactic is to give up some of the net on the side that the puck carrier is coming down, hoping to sucker him to shoot to that area instead of passing. If you choose this strategy, of course, you must be able to react extremely quickly should the puck carrier take advantage of the opening.

When practicing 2-on-0, the players should come at different speeds, angles, and positions. Explain to your coach the importance of seeing variation in the drill so you can experiment with new situations and bring your game to a new level.

THE THREE-ON-TWO

Playing a 3-on-2 situation requires preparation and anticipation. The goaltender must rely on many different skills, for there are many possible scenarios.

Your first priority, as always, is the puck carrier. He has the option to shoot or go hard to the net and try to deke the defenseman. Play the angles as if he will shoot; but don't come out too far or he will pass the puck behind you, leaving an open net for either teammate.

Usually one opponent will be going hard to the net while the other positions himself in an open area. If the puck goes to the high man, you should adjust by executing a quick hip rotation and an aggressive forward/lateral shuffle. If the shooter slides a drop pass behind him, don't use only a lateral adjustment, as this will give the new shooter more net to look at. Also, you must be aggressive if the puck carrier attempts to pass the puck to his teammate going to the net. Don't back away from the confrontation, thus allowing him to deflect or one-time the puck into an open net. Use the strategies as discussed later ("The Deflection," page 150). Intercept the pass if you can; or get right on top of where the tip or redirection may come from. Don't stay too deep in your crease.

It is imperative that you know your defensemen, and that you all understand how you will play any situation *as a group*. Don't be afraid to shout instructions to your teammates.

If your defenseman takes the opponent going to the net, you are in a 2-on-1 situation; as in any 2-on-1, you want the player with the lowest percentages to shoot the puck. If you have the puck carrier isolated on a tough angle, shout this to your teammates so they know that the pass is their responsibility because you are aggressively playing the carrier.

In practice don't just run through twenty 3-on-2 situations without talking and strategizing with your defensemen. Make sure everyone, from the coach to the sixth defenseman, understands and is in agreement on the strategy you are using. Reflexes can only take you so far. A smart goaltender playing in synchrony with his teammates can significantly diminish the number of big opportunities for his opponents.

GAME SITUATIONS

This section provides specific strategies to use in specific game situations. I urge you to read through the following paragraphs as many times as will be required for you to internalize what you learn.

Defending Against the Centering Pass

The centering pass is one that comes from the corner or behind the net to a player standing in scoring position. You must give yourself the best chance to stop the puck by getting there as fast as possible.

Your first task is to rotate your hips so you are attacking with the biggest part of your body going at the puck. It is in this circumstance that you should use your power move to aggressively attack the point where the opponent will release the shot. The assumption is that the player is going to one-time the puck. Remember to stop your forward progress and set for the shot just in case the shooter hesitates, bobbles the puck, or decides to deke.

Your goal is to get as far out on your angle as you can without risking too much, and to allow yourself time to set and therefore react to the shot. A good strategy for bigger goalies is to get to the middle of the net from the post as quickly as possible, and then move out

Figure 6.4 Get out on top of the shot.

when the shooter is in front of the net. This allows you to take advantage of your size.

Charging a Loose Puck

One of the most exciting plays in hockey occurs when a forward and an opposing goaltender are racing for a loose puck. The most important thing for the goaltender to remember is that if she hesitates she is doomed. The decision to charge should be made in an instant; if it isn't, hold up and play out the scenario.

If the race is close, try to smother the puck with your glove rather than taking a swipe at it with your stick. Once you have the puck smothered, tuck your glove into your body and cover that area with your stick and blocker, just in case the puck is squeezed out. When trapping the puck, make sure to back up your glove with the stick. The benefit of freezing the puck is that you don't risk making a bad play with your stick (and you'll also boost your confidence by enjoying the applause and attention as the whistle blows!).

If you get to the puck early, you will have to make a play with your stick. There are three things to keep in mind in this case:

- Make an easy pass if that is feasible—remember, you have left your net wide open and losing control of the puck will leave you helpless.
- Try to pass on the same side that you are on: a cross-ice pass is risky. If your team loses control, at least you will be on the same side as the puck and can try to regain your angle on the way back.
- If you have no one to pass to, fire the puck off the glass or against the boards closest to you. Make sure the puck clears the blue line, as this will catch the player you raced for the puck offside and leave you valuable seconds to return to your net.

You can use the last-mentioned tactic to clear the puck from your own zone. Aim for a spot off the glass just inside the blue line. By clearing the puck you will trap the opposing forwards offside, forcing them to regroup and allowing your team to implement its neutral zone forecheck.

Low Corner Positioning

When opponents attack from low in the corner, goaltenders often get caught in a positioning error. Generally you should be square to the

Figure 6.5 Always play the shooter first.

puck, but this rule changes when the opposing player is behind the goal line; here you must switch to behind-the-net positioning.

Your pads, hips, and chest should all be square to the puck as long as the opponent has a shot on net. Don't assume he is going to take the puck deeper. Only when he has passed the point where he can no longer cut back in front of the net should you move both feet back to the goal line.

Defensive Zone Face-Offs

Position yourself at the point where the rectangular crease connects with the semicircular one. Make sure you have a clear sight on the puck. Have your center always check to see if you are ready before she sets to take the draw.

Know what your centers like to do in defensive zone face-offs. Consider their weaknesses and estimate the probable direction of the puck. Scan your defensive alignment and the offensive setup. By noting the position of the players and the way they shoot, you can predict their first and second option shooters. A well-coached team will have different offensive zone alignments based on personnel and game situations. Preparing for a particular situation and planning your response before it happens will lead to quicker and more confident reactions when it does happen.

ANTICIPATION

The words anticipation and guessing often are confused in the world of goaltending. A *guess* means the goaltender has no clue where the puck is heading and moves in desperation before the shot is released. *Anticipation* is when a goaltender picks up clues by reading the shooter's eyes, posture, and positioning; considers the mechanics involved in the release and follow-through of the shot; then acts as the puck is being released.

Whether consciously or unconsciously, a goaltender will notice characteristics of a shot as it is being taken. After the sequence is completed time and time again, the goalie's reaction will become automatic, increasing his speed in intercepting the puck.

Figure 6.6 Don't get caught anticipating the pass.

Here are eight tips on anticipation. Watch and mentally record the following:

1. ***The head and eyes.*** Although a good scorer keeps her head up as she shoots, many players tip off the goaltender by their head movement. Often a player will approach the net with his head down, stickhandling the puck; he lifts his head to see what net there is to shoot at; then when he looks down again, you know the shot is coming and where he wants to shoot it!

2. ***Posture.*** The posture of the shooter gives you a good idea of the height he will be able to get on his shot. A player standing erect will have a tough time getting height on the puck. A player who is compact in his release will have an easier time putting the puck upstairs.

3. ***Distance between player and puck.*** If the puck is lying far away from the shooter, it is difficult for her to roll her wrists and "pull" the puck from this position. Power (and therefore speed) will be detracted from her shot, and she will have difficulty getting the puck up top with any velocity. In this situation, the player may slap at the puck; or, if she does see open net high, she may elect to chop at it. Anticipate a low shot with a path leading away from the shooter.

The player has better options when he pulls the puck in toward his body before his release. Often he will be looking for a quick shot, middle to high net. A good tactic for the shooter is to bring the puck in tight (looking to go short side for example), pulling the goaltender to one side, and firing at the five-hole or away from his body.

4. ***The shoulders.*** The shooter's shoulders and their rotation can give you a solid clue to where the puck will be heading. The lead shoulder is the key: if the player wants to shoot on an inside path, or "pull" the puck, she is going to bring that shoulder across her body. The more dramatically the shoulder comes across, the more surely you can anticipate the puck following its lead.

5. ***Angle of the blade.*** When a player strikes a puck, the angle of the stick blade can show you where he is shooting. If the blade is open as the stick strikes the puck, anticipate the puck's going away from the shooter's body. If he rolls his wrists forward and the blade closes on the puck, it should head inside of the shooter's body.

6. ***Point of release.*** Look for the release point of the shot (when the puck leaves the blade). The farther back the release point, the

greater the likelihood that the puck will stay low. The farther the puck is in front of the shooter when she releases, the greater the probability that the puck will go high.

7. ***The follow-through.*** If the player stays low on his release and follows through, the puck will probably stay low on its path to the net. If the blade of the stick doesn't follow through high, neither will the puck. If the shooter pulls his head and chest up through the shot, the trajectory will probably be to the upper corners.

8. ***Options.*** Anticipate the options available to the shooter. A perfect example is when a player swings the net on her forehand. Originally her shot will come low because the puck is ahead of her body; but if given time to pull up and bring the puck in tight, her best option will be to go upstairs. Know what situations produce what options for the shooter, and prepare yourself.

Because games move so fast, you cannot consciously read all the available clues. But if you know the clues described above and practice reading them, your game will improve dramatically because you eventually will be able to register the clues automatically.

A good goal scorer knows that you're picking up signals from the way he shoots. He therefore disguises his clues to make you think the puck will go in one direction when he is actually shooting in another. He will do this by throwing a shoulder, not rolling his wrists when he releases, or even having an unconventional curve in his stick. Use anticipation as an added skill, not a crutch.

goalies' tip

Sometimes the puck hits a slight rut or bump in the ice just as a player is about to shoot, and it begins to flutter. I call this a "scared puck." Because the puck is not lying flat, your ability to predict where it is heading is severely diminished. The best strategy for handling this situation is to be aggressive. Move out on the angle and maintain a compact stance. You are playing the percentages of the shot hitting your body or missing the net. The flight of the puck will not be what the shooter intends and will likely go high. The closer you are, the less chance you have of being hit in the head or shoulders and getting hurt.

ERIN WHITTEN

Erin Whitten is a winner. Not only did she lead the University of New Hampshire women Wildcats to two Eastern Collegiate Athletic Conference Championships in 1989-90 and 1990-91, but she was also named the ECAC goaltender of the year for all four seasons she played. Whitten was the USA National Women's team goaltender from 1992-97, playing in three World Championships, and winning the 1993 Olympic Festival and the Three Nations Cup. Her skill and dedication to women's hockey continuously raised the level of play, culminating in the USA beating Canada for the gold medal in the 1998 Olympics.

Whitten's philosophy in challenging the shooter is to combine patience and aggressiveness. "If you are overly aggressive you might get caught too far out of your crease, but if you are too patient you may show too much of the net." Great goaltenders know when to challenge aggressively and when to let the play come to them. When asked about whether girls should play with the boys' team or with the girls' program, Whitten has some super advice. "Stick with the program that will help you develop and where you will have fun playing the game. Whichever program you choose, concentrate on practicing the basics and always strive to get better."

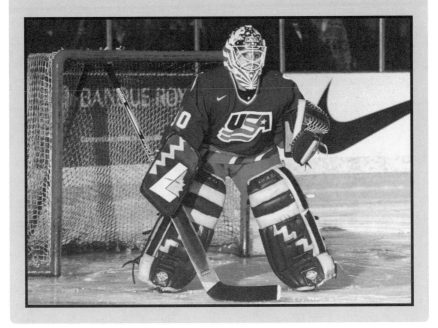

CONTROLLING REBOUNDS

You can drastically reduce the number of shots on net you receive by improving your ability to control rebounds. Anytime you're practicing a drill with long shots, practice also your ability to analyze the puck's trajectory and to anticipate where it will end up.

Clear Shots

Whenever possible, catch a shot with the glove. A shot saved by the blocker should be either trapped or steered to the corner. Remember to tilt your blocker downward to place the puck under control.

If you are rotating your hips and shoulders, the puck should end up to the left or the right of the crease. Kick saves executed properly allow you to steer the puck to either corner. Remember to rotate your hips, allowing the angle of your pad to dictate the direction the puck will take. Your stick blade can redirect a shot along the ice. A simple stab with the stick in either direction may save that extra second it would take to perform a kick save.

One of the most difficult shots to control is one about 1 1/2 feet to 3 feet off the ice, right down the middle. The ideal save would be

Figure 6.7   There is no need to give them another opportunity.

a glove save that would control the play. Most likely you will be pulling your legs together to shut the five-hole. If you are fortunate to trap the puck between your pads, place your hand over this area and get the whistle.

If you are going to leave a rebound, bend your knees forward over your toes, directing the puck downward and to an area you can smother. If the puck is to the left or right, drive into the shot, adjusting the angle of the pad and directing the puck to the corner.

A great help in improving your control is to follow the puck right through the save with your eyes. Many goaltenders have the habit of taking their eyes off the biscuit. If the puck lands in front of you on the ice, cover it as quickly as possible. Drop to your glove side knee. Place your glove over the puck and your stick in front—the stick will provide protection against someone's taking a swipe at your hand.

Figure 6.8 Tom prepares to smother the puck after the save.

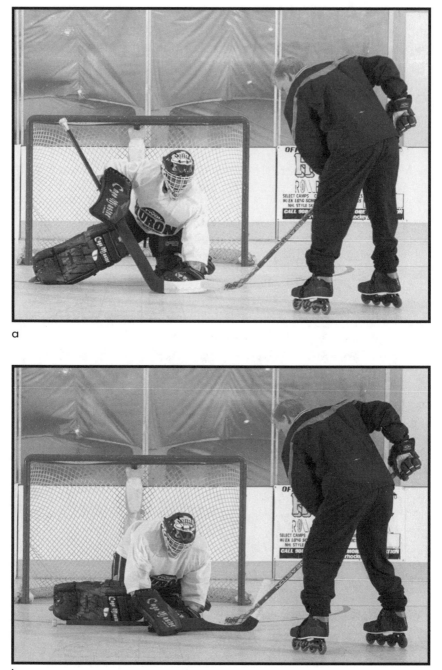

a

b

Figure 6.9a-b   Protect your fingers by placing the blade of your stick in front of your glove.

The Screen Shot

With the size of players and speed of the game constantly increasing, goaltenders find themselves relying more on their positioning and fundamentals and less on pure reflexes. Facing a shot that comes through a screen is like playing goal blindfolded.

The first thing you want to do is work hard to spot the biscuit without taking yourself out of position. Try to stay centered to where the shot is coming from. If an opposing player is positioned in front of you, stay low and look to her right or left. Use your glove hand to move her in the opposite direction from where you want to look—for example, if you want to look to her left, push her left hip with your glove toward her right side. Try to stay on your feet as long as possible and keep your stick on the ice. Never look over your opponent's shoulder in a screen situation: it lifts your stick off the ice and reduces the bend in your knees, making it difficult to make the save if the puck is launched.

You will hear or feel the shot being released. In this scenario most goalies will drop to their knees and cover the ice so as not to allow a soft goal—this means either a butterfly or a shaft down. When you go down, remember to remain as "big" as possible by keeping your chest and hands high. Once you are down, you have minimal chance of getting back into position after the shot—so be sure to smother the puck or otherwise control the rebound.

If you are inhibited from freely moving around the goal mouth, your ability to play angles and challenge the shooter will decrease. A goaltender must stake his claim to his crease, and new regulations are helping. There are several ways to discourage players from hanging in front of your net. If you are going to use your stick to intimidate a player, remember that you don't want it off the ice for too long. A quick, short slash to the ankle area will send the appropriate message without costing your team. You want your opponent to realize that you have the ability to hurt her, and to give you more room to work.

Sometimes a goaltender will be screened because of a pileup of players that forces her deep in the crease. One way to escape this potentially dangerous situation is to dislodge the net by lifting the crossbar with your shoulders; another is to fall back into one of the posts as though shoved. Of course you can be called for delay of game, so you'll need to call upon your best acting ability. If this is a strategy you like to use, you should loosen the net by lifting the crossbar with your shoulders before the start of every period so the posts are not frozen rock solid into the ice.

Figure 6.10   Move opposing forwards out of the way by pushing their hips.

The Deflection

Working on deflections is not every goalie's preference, but it is essential. The unpredictability of the direction of the shot increases the risk of injury to the goaltender. Make sure that your neck and shoulder areas are well protected, because the trajectory of the puck increases radically when it is deflected close to the net.

If the puck is deflected well out from the goal crease, you can rely on your reflexes to make the save. But when a puck is tipped in front of the net, positioning is essential. The key to playing a deflected shot is aggressiveness. You want to move as much of your body as possible toward the spot where the puck is deflected. If you can, stay on your feet and stop right where the shot will be tipped. A powerful T-glide or shuffle will get you there quickly. Don't glide over—explode to the spot.

If you can't get there standing, use one of the suggested saves. Your opponent can tip the puck in many directions, so be careful to cut down the angle on a tipped shot the same way you play the angles on a shooter. Unfortunately, you have far less time to react to a tipped shot than to a shot from farther out.

If you can, play the original shot or pass. If you can get your stick on the puck before it gets tipped, you're in good shape. A goaltender who sits back in his net and relies solely on his reflexes in this situation will hurt his own percentages of stopping the puck. A save on a deflection often results in a rebound: be conscious of this fact and you will react more quickly when it occurs. Pounce on the loose puck or clear it with your stick, because there will be an opponent on your front doorstep.

Figure 6.11 Don't get distracted. Anticipate the shot coming on net.

Figure 6.12 The key is getting as close to the deflection or tip as possible.

Figure 6.13 By going down, you take away anything along the ice.

HOW WILL YOU REACT?

Practice the material in this chapter until it is second nature to you. Your best chance to make the save means that you must challenge, follow, and square up with the shooter.

Imagine this scenario: *an opposing player crosses center ice with the puck and then heads outside the defenseman and drives to the deep right corner.* Now ask yourself if you could react as described below.

1. As the player moves toward your zone, take a power stride forward to challenge the shot.

2. When he cuts outside to go around the defenseman, do not follow his course by skating backwards with your hips facing right. Review the section on "Hip Rotation" in chapter 4: if the player is moving to your right, rotate your hips to the left.

3. Once your hips are rotated, power shuffle along an arc, tracking the opponent's path. Because of proper hip rotation you should always be squared to the shooter; and because you are moving in an arc rather than laterally, the player will not gain a better scoring advantage as he enters the zone.

4. When the player arrives in the corner, use backward C-cuts to move to the post. If the player beats the defenseman and drives to the net, you will be at a perfect angle and depth to challenge him; and you'll have room to skate backward while the player approaches without ending up too deep in your crease.

A mistake many goaltenders make when following a player entering the zone to either side is skating backward before hip rotation and adjustment. The goaltender is thus never square to the shooter, and his shoulders tend to face center ice rather than the opposing player.

Remember, the first move you make is to rotate your hips; only then should you move to challenge or follow.

7

Controlling the Puck

As the position of goaltender evolves, so do some of its demands. Today's goaltender must be able to handle the puck to aid his team in breaking out of the zone. There is often little time in practice to concentrate on this skill, so it is up to the goaltender to utilize any down time to work on passing and clearing the puck.

SET UP

Properly setting up a dumped-in puck can be a big help to the defense. You should always leave the puck flat and in an area that does not limit the options of your defensemen.

When the puck is shot along the ice, your first job is to control the dump-in before trying to set it up. The easiest way to do this is to drop your glove hand knee to the ice and place your glove behind the stick blade. The glove acts as a buffer for the stick and provides security if the biscuit jumps.

Figure 7.1 Use your glove as a backup in case the puck jumps.

With the puck under control, place it to either side of the net. Leave the puck just ahead of the goal line and one foot outside the edge of the crease. By leaving the puck away from the net, you limit the risk of your defensemen accidentally shooting the puck into your own net; this is also a position where, if something happens to the defenseman, you can smother the puck or shoot it yourself. By picking a spot outside the crease you leave your defenseman the option of cutting behind the net or skating into the corner.

Avoid stopping the puck on one side of the net and placing it on another, because it can be confusing to your own players. Often when your team forwards come back, they are tired. Or they may have bad habits and put their heads down as they skate back. In either case they may not see that you've switched sides.

Don't pass the puck to the location where you want to leave it. Rather, lead it with your stick and set it—it requires a little extra work, but the defense will feel comfortable knowing that the puck will always be waiting for them at a specific spot.

Figure 7.2   Set the puck. Just pushing it to the side is not doing your job.

If a puck is dumped in very quickly to your blocker side, use the proper technique as previously described. Turning your stick blade over and hoping to control the shot is dangerous, and a sign of a lazy goaltender.

If the puck is dumped in to your glove side too far away to stop with conventional means, you can cover the extra distance by dropping your blocker side knee to the ice and laying your stick flat along the ice. Recover and set the puck up at the correct spot by using your backhand. Do not attempt to imitate this move to the other side.

If the puck is traveling away from the net on your blocker side, play it safe and let the puck go as deep as the goal line. Slide your blocker up the shaft of the stick and hold firmly for excess reach while turning your stick over. Stop the puck using the back of the blade, then set it in position. If you are stopping these dump-ins by just turning your stick over and maintaining your grip on the handle, you are taking the easy way out.

Figure 7.3   Don't take risks, but help your defensemen out as much as possible.

If the puck is fired too hard for you to control, let it carom off the dasher board, and stop it as it returns toward the goal line.

High Dump-In

When an opponent flicks a high dump-in in front of the net, you never know which way the puck will bounce. Play the puck, don't let it play you. The ideal situation would be to move out and catch the puck before it lands. If this is not possible, move as close to the landing spot as possible, placing yourself in a tight stance with your knees bent forward to control the rebound. If the puck is going to bounce well out in front of the net, stay put and react to the bounce—don't get caught out of your net in an unpredictable situation.

Controlling the Puck Behind the Net

You need timing and confidence, which come only with practice, to become skilled at stopping a puck dumped in behind your net. A team whose goaltender is weak in this skill will be forechecked harder than one whose goaltender is consistently able to help take control in these situations.

TECHNIQUE #1

From his stance, a goalkeeper must be able to explode toward the back of the net to the left or right of the posts. Some goalies use a T-glide, while others use one or two crossovers for that extra jump.

Arriving at the boards on your glove hand will leave you with two approaches. The most secure is to press against the boards with the outside of your pad and the tip of your stick. Your position should be similar to the basic stance, but with the glove closed and pressed against the boards. Angle your stick blade toward the boards so the puck doesn't ricochet out front.

Placing the glove this way controls your approach into the boards and generates power as you push off with your arm, helping you return quickly to your crease. Once you control the puck, use the tip of the stick blade to pull it off the boards where either the defenseman can easily play it or you can clear it. Return quickly to your crease on the same side you exited.

Be sure your defensemen understand that they should never cut between you and the net when going back to retrieve a puck. This can lead to accidental contact and chaos.

Figure 7.4   Use your glove as a shock absorber and a spring.

Figure 7.5   Make sure the defense knows you have the inside track back to your net.

Figure 7.6 Marc is ready to fire the puck as soon as he gets it.

If you are playing on a quality ice surface and/or you don't have enough time to get to the boards, you can stop the puck by setting up as if you were a forward receiving a pass. You will be able to move the puck quickly using this technique, but be careful because the puck may take an unpredictable carom off the boards, leaving you out of position. Try to be proficient in both techniques.

STRATEGY A: If forecheckers prevent you from leaving the puck for your defenseman, you should shoot using a forehand or backhand. By using the forehand, you shoot the puck in the direction you are facing—permitting you to follow its path and return to the net on the same side the puck lies. In using the backhand, you take a chance by shooting the puck to an area you can't see—and you may have to return to the net from the opposite side from where the puck lies.

Regardless of what side you fire the puck, try to get it high off the glass. This will afford you a few extra seconds to return to your net.

goalies' tip

STRATEGY B: Sometimes you will be in position on your glove side when a puck comes off the boards about six inches away from the boards. Ideally you would like to control it and set for the defenseman, but you're concerned that the spin on the puck will lead it to carom off your stick and back into play. In this situation try angling your stick toward the boards to deflect the puck. With proper timing, you can make the puck come off the base of the dasher (bottom of the boards) and stop in perfect position for your teammate to retrieve it, while you hustle back to your net.

TECHNIQUE #2

There is not as much security in stopping the puck behind the net to your blocker side. Before you reach the boards, you should be in your stance facing the direction the puck is coming from. Turn your stick over and place the tip inward against the dasher board. After you control the puck, pull it away from the boards so your defenseman can easily gain control, and hustle back to the crease on the same side you exited. If you have to play the puck, use the same forehand or backhand technique described previously.

Figure 7.7 Remember not to turn your back on the play.

goalies' tip

One of the cardinal rules of goaltending is to always face the play. When stopping the puck behind the net do not turn your back to the rest of the ice surface.

STRATEGY A: Whether you stop the puck behind the net on your glove side or blocker side, do not venture directly behind the middle of the net. If a bad bounce occurs, you can be left stranded. Also, when the defenseman goes to pick up the puck with a forechecker tight on his heels, you may be caught in a traffic jam with limited room to return to the crease.

STRATEGY B: Never exit your crease on the side opposite that on which the puck is dumped. You probably have seen enough blooper videos to know that the glass and boards are not always true and can send the puck in strange directions!

SHOOTING THE PUCK

Not everyone can handle the puck like Ron Hextall. Being able to pass the puck well, however, may mean the difference between being a starter or second stringer. Be sure to use the right stick—one that will not inhibit your shooting skills. Chapter 1 provides tips for selecting a stick.

Forehand Technique

Goaltenders shoot pucks much as other players do. Grip the shaft of the stick comfortably with your glove, and grip the knob of your stick with the blocker. Most goaltenders shoot off the inside leg, making it easier to lift the puck.

Start with the puck at the heel of your blade and behind your body. Generate momentum by pulling your arms and shoulders forward and bending slightly at the knees and waist. As the puck crosses the center of the blade, roll your wrists and release the puck.

Don't flick your shot by releasing way ahead of your body. The power comes from leaning into the shot and being over the puck.

RON HEXTALL

When Ron Hextall came to the NHL no one predicted what an effect he would have on the position. His ability to shoot and handle the puck was at a higher level than any previously seen. This dimension of his game proved to be such an asset to the Philadelphia Flyers that all coaches began putting more pressure on their goaltenders to work on their puck handling skills. Nowadays coaches believe that a goalie who can handle the biscuit isn't just a great asset, but a necessity. Part of Hextall's ability rests in his choice of stick—although he uses a considerable curve, the key is his dramatic rocker. When he is in his stance and the blade lies on the ice, there is actually very little of the blade that touches the ice. This rocker allows him to get maximum height on his shot. By lifting the puck easier, he is able to bank it off the glass and clear the zone, and in 1989 Hextall even scored an NHL playoff goal!

© Rick Berk/Bruce Bennett Studios

Figure 7.8 For a long pass, you may get more power by shooting off your lead foot.

Because many goaltenders are overly concerned about the height of the puck, they neglect working on power and consistently shoot floaters that are easily picked off.

Goaltenders are beginning to realize the benefits of shooting off their front foot as well as their back. You can shoot harder by using the technique illustrated in figure 7.8. It is very useful when you want to make a long pass to center ice while keeping the puck low. When you want to play the puck off the glass, it's better to shoot off your inside foot.

goalies' tip

Figure 7.9   Whenever possible, practice handling and firing the puck.

Backhand Technique

Slide your blocker and grab the knob of your stick firmly. Find a comfortable place for your glove along the shaft, where you feel in control. Apply the same principles to the backhand as you did to the forehand, remembering to start your movement with the puck behind your body and not to pull your body out of the shot. Keep the puck to the center of the blade.

Even though goaltenders rarely use a backhand shot, it is an excellent skill to possess. How often do you see a goalie create chaos by trying to clear the puck out of danger with a bad backhand? Being able to ring a backhand around the glass is a great way to control a difficult situation.

goalies' tip   If you have a chance before or after practice, throw a bunch of pucks in the high slot. Practice shooting the pucks over the crossbar and against the glass using both forehand and backhand techniques. Remember to stress power rather than just floating the pucks.

Stickhandling

Stickhandling is merely moving the puck from your forehand to your backhand. The key is to control the puck by cupping it with the blade of the stick. Goaltenders should join the other players in as many skating and stickhandling drills as possible.

COVERAGE BEHIND THE NET

Although players score few goals from behind the net, it is an area where many scoring opportunities are initiated. Being able to cover an opponent in this position can help you intercept passes and deny the opportunity for players to walk out in front of the net.

Positioning

When covering a man behind your glove side post, get the outside heel of your skate up against the inside of the post and run your pad up

Figure 7.10   Use your glove to catch any lofted centering passes.

the pipe. Remember to bend at the waist in proper stance. Bring the stick to the same side as the glove and turn the blade over—this is the key to blocking centering passes. Place the blade as close to the goal line as possible. If the blade is too far out, an intercepted pass may deflect between your legs and into the net. Turn your glove over, outside the post, and face the palm open to the shooter. Use the glove to intercept passes that may be lifted over your stick.

goalies' tip   The best way to get from post to post is to use a power shuffle. The worst thing you can do is execute an easy glide. If the puck reverses direction while you are in your glide you may have a difficult time readjusting.

When covering a man over your blocker shoulder, align your heel and pad as you do on your glove side. Place your stick behind the goal line so that the blade produces an arc for intercepting passes. Hold the stick upright, not allowing it to tilt inward—you don't want the knob of the stick to be obstructed by the netting. Bring your glove across your body, prepared to catch pucks lofted across the crease.

Figure 7.11   Make sure to keep the stick free and the knob away from the netting.

It is usually best to hold your stick out in position, denying a passing lane to the player behind the net. There are times, however, when you see the play develop and can anticipate exactly what the path of the pass will be. At these times you may want to keep your stick cocked tight to your body, allowing your opponent to attempt the pass, then thrusting the blade out to intercept the puck.

It is always quicker to push your stick in an outward motion than it is to pull it inward.

goalies' tip

Movement Behind the Net

Covering a player setting up behind the net is no easy task. Traditionally, goaltenders have held their posts, and as opponents moved out of view, the goalies picked them up over their opposite shoulders. For example: if a player approached from your glove side and went behind the net, you would hold the post on that side—and as he drifted to the middle of the cage, you would turn your head to look over your blocker side shoulder.

Figure 7.12 Try to keep the shooter over your glove shoulder.

Today's goaltenders, however, are less inclined than yesterday's to lose sight of the player. Instead of immediately switching vision from shoulder to shoulder, try drifting off your post, maintaining eye contact with the puck. You'll find that you never lose sight of the puck as the player sets up behind the net, so a quick reverse pass can't strand you. I recommend this tactic especially when you're following a player over your glove shoulder—it's easier to keep your body square to the ice and ready to react to the centering pass than if you were looking over your other shoulder.

HANGING THE STICK

This strategy is very risky and only applicable in certain situations; but the results may surprise you. Often you'll find yourself alone on your blocker side against an opponent who has all day to pick her spot. Instead of feeling at the shooter's mercy, you may want to play aggressively—hoping to surprise the shooter and force her either to hurry or to try something she doesn't really want to do.

You can press the shooter by hanging your stick out with the blade close to the puck. Now your opponent has little ice on which to

Figure 7.13   Although an aggressive move, this strategy may surprise the shooter and defuse a dangerous situation.

maneuver the puck, pressuring him to make a quick decision and allowing your defense to close in. The key is to stay on your feet and maintain a strong grip on the shaft, keeping the blade right on top of the puck. You stand a great opportunity of poking the puck away, or at least of blocking the shot with your stick because of the height your opponent needs to clear your blade at that distance.

goalies' tip

You can also try this move with a player (sweeping in) from the blocker side. Continue your backward motion as the player approaches, while hanging your stick out. You will restrict the area she has to maneuver the puck, possibly forcing her to a make a mistake.

This is a very aggressive move for goaltenders. Practice it often; don't try it in a game situation till you feel very confident with it.

TAKE CHARGE!

Unfortunately, not many practice drills focus on the goaltender. It is your responsibility to make sure that you handle the puck in every practice; that you practice reading shooters' intentions and making quick decisions; and that you interact appropriately with your teammates. Don't wait for the coach to cater to your needs: he has twenty other players to work with, and may not have as much time as he would like to help goaltenders.

8

Developing a
Shutout Mindset

There comes a point in an athlete's career when she has to look at herself for motivation. When you were a child, your coaches and parents were always there to pick you up and give you a push when you needed it. Moving ahead often requires leaving security behind— even a screaming coach will motivate you only for so long.

MENTAL TOUGHNESS

Not all coaches have the same strategy in preparing a team, and not all goaltenders have the same mental approach to the game. Some goalies like to be all fired up and mad at the world when they compete; others prefer to play in a calm and conservative manner. You can't tell other people what their approach should be, but you can help them see some of the factors that can contribute to their success.

A self-evaluation is part of the goal-setting form at the end of this chapter. Be sure to note on your self-evaluation what state of mind you had at the beginning of the game in question, and throughout the game. By analyzing these forms, you will likely find that you consistently play at a higher level when you compete in a specific state of mind. Prepare a list of emotions you have when you are in this particular state. Go over this list before the game, and see if you can place yourself on this emotional level.

goalies' tip

Athletes are often notorious for their rituals and superstitions. Players may have to eat the same meal before every game, or park their cars at specific spots. For players who have such superstitions, following through on them can help induce the right frame of mind for playing the game. Patrick Roy, for example, will not skate over the blue lines while skating to and from his net—he actually hops over them. This little ritual, performed only at game time, helps him stay concentrated and in the zone.

COACH-GOALTENDER RELATIONS

A goaltender's needs are very specific, and different from those of the rest of the team. Open communication between coach and goalie is extremely important. Players often are too intimidated to discuss problems with their coaches. To be successful in this competitive position, however, you must do everything possible to improve your performance—and that may require confronting the coach.

Most coaches were not goaltenders themselves, and sometimes they have trouble grasping the concepts and mentality of goaltending. It is up to you to become knowledgeable on the fundamentals by watching tapes and reading manuals such as this one. Then, if there is a point the coach is missing, it is up to you to explain it.

There are appropriate and inappropriate times to approach your coach with suggestions. To be successful, he must have the players' respect and discipline—so if you believe a practice drill is counterproductive to you, don't express your feelings there on the ice. Wait until after practice and sit down with the coach *in private* when he'll have an open mind and time to analyze your suggestions. *Never* question his skill or judgment in front of the other players!—the last thing you want is to back him into a corner. Even in your private conversations, always leave him a dignified way out of a controversial situation. After you've talked with him, don't keep bugging him. Give him time to set the drill up differently for the next training session. After that practice, if you can tell he still doesn't grasp the concept, bring him the tape or manual with the explanation and present it to him in a respectful manner.

There must be mutual respect between you and your coach. Show her you want to learn and improve your game by working 100 percent in practices and games. Demonstrate your desire to do everything possible, including analyzing practices and games with her and discussing what can be changed to make things better for you.

Always show a willingness to play in all circumstances. Never project a lack of self-confidence to your coach, even if you are in a state of low self-esteem. This will reduce the confidence level the coach has in you and make her decision easier to go with the other goaltender. Never look to the bench after a goal. Get ready to play again and shake it off. If the coach yanks you, skate to the bench with your head high and get motivated for your next chance to play. Don't lumber to the bench hanging your head like a defeated person, as this will negatively affect the morale of your entire team. If you don't agree with a move, don't pout on the bench; rather, encourage the other players and goaltender. After the following practice where you've worked 100 percent, respectfully discuss with the coach why you were pulled and what you need to work on to improve your standing in her eyes.

goalies' tip Many goaltenders get caught up worrying about the game, and it drains them physically. Break the game into three parts and have players think about the score after each period. This breaks the contest into three short games, each with a distinct beginning and ending. Goalies get a break after each period, and are ready to start the "next game" with a fresh outlook.

Perhaps the most discouraging thing for a coach and her players to see is a beaten goaltender. After a goal, avoid lying on the ice or shaking your head. Let the referee pull the puck from the net, and either go for a brief skate or get back immediately to your set position. Keep your chest and head held high and show that you're ready to compete. Reacting this way puts you back into the correct mental state and makes your teammates feel secure.

BEING THE QUARTERBACK

Picture yourself at one end of a mine field with the task of getting to the other end. You have to move, even though you know one wrong step will be a big mistake. That creates a lot of tension, to say the least.

Now imagine how you would feel if someone were telling you where the mines are. You'd be a lot more confident!

A good goalie does everything he can to help his team, and that includes talking to his teammates during the play. Be quick to yell out when you are screened; also be quick to yell instructions to a defenseman when she is retrieving a puck: "MAN ON!" or "YOU HAVE TIME!" or some other appropriate phrase. If you see an easy outlet pass, let her know; and if she has time to skate, shout "WHEEL!" or "GO WITH IT!" If you see the other team dump it in for a line change, let your defenseman know—she may have pivoted quickly and didn't recognize this. Defensemen spend a lot of time skating with their backs to the play, so you've got to be the eyes in the back of their heads.

You can aid your team immensely by talking on the ice. Not only does it help your teammates make correct decisions, it demonstrates leadership and confidence. The players appreciate the help, and it reinforces to them that their goalie is on top of the game.

> You are not the only player responsible for talking to teammates. When you go behind the net to stop a puck, it is essential that your defense yells whether you should leave it or move it. However, it is your responsibility that they understand this. **goalies' tip**

GOALTENDER COMPETITION

Through tryouts, the regular season, and the playoffs you will be competing for playing time with other goalies. There is often jealousy and conflict, with players even lobbying for one goaltender or the other.

Competition is essential for you to reach your maximum potential. Welcome the challenge, and realize you will improve more by being pushed then if you had no pressure. Don't take the challenge on a personal level; your competition wants to play hockey and be successful just like you. The starting job should be won on the ice— not by backstabbing and politics, which disrupt the chemistry of the team and lead to bickering and disharmony. You have a responsibility to yourself, your coach, and your teammates to do everything you can

BYRON DAFOE

When the Boston Bruins obtained Byron Dafoe from the Los Angeles Kings on August 29, 1997, they told him they wanted competition for the number one goaltending job. Considering that the Bruins already had Jim Carey and his 2.2 million dollar salary, not too many people expected Dafoe to see much action. Carey was the 1995-96 Vezina Trophy winner with the Washington Capitals, the same team Dafoe had made ten appearances with over two seasons, and the Bruins had dealt their starting goaltender Bill Ranford in the deal that brought Carey to Boston. Despite his tag as "back-up," Dafoe battled to earn playing time and eventually won the starting job. The 26-year-old backup goaltender played his way into the number one spot during the 1997-98 season despite the odds against him. The Bruins even ended up sending Carey to the minors, making Dafoe the undisputed number one goalie in the organization. If Byron Dafoe had come to the Boston Bruins re-signed to the fact he was going to be number two, he never would have earned the starting job. When you are not the starter, you always have to stay physically and mentally alert because you never know when you are going to be given the chance to show what you can do!

© J. Leary/Bruce Bennett Studios

to help the team win, whether by starting or being prepared to come off the bench.

Because goaltenders play a unique position, there is usually a bonding among a team's goalies. I hope that, if you are on a team with two or three goaltenders, you will experience relationships of mutual respect. Even if there is tension among you, try to maintain the highest level of professionalism. By watching another goaltender practice and play throughout the season, you pick up habits from him. Analyze his game completely and borrow from his repertoire aspects that will improve your style. You can mutually raise the level of your play by acting as each other's goalie coaches and pointing out positive and negative points in each other's game. By doing this, you raise the quality of the entire team. An adverse relationship among competing goaltenders will only distract and detract from your potential improvement.

OVERCOMING NERVOUSNESS

Nervousness is a sensation that all goaltenders experience. It can slow your reflexes and lead to bad decisions. If you are scared to make a mistake, you will hesitate; and that hesitation can translate into a goal. You must learn to translate your nervous energy into power.

Three Keys to Overcoming Nervousness

There are three keys to beating a case of nerves: practice, focus, and attitude.

PRACTICE

Remember the nervous feeling you had when you went into an exam for which you only studied the previous night? Was the feeling different when you had prepared adequately? An honest player who works 100 percent at practice is a player with integrity. Integrity translates into respect for yourself, and that respect translates into confidence. Self-confidence and pride will defeat a bout of the nerves.

In practice, you have the chance to prepare your response to many different situations. By thinking about how you will play certain situations and knowing what to do before they even happen, you will develop much quicker reaction times when they do happen. Practice is not just physical: *think the position!*

FOCUS

You cannot perform to the best of your ability without concentration. Your state of concentration must remain constant throughout the game, without lapses. Often a bad goal can open the floodgates, or a bad game can cause a slump. A successful approach to deal with events that can break concentration is to focus on future results. If you know the results you are looking for down the road, you'll find it easier to deal with minor setbacks.

coaches' tip

Sometimes goaltenders get overwhelmed with all the decisions they will need to make throughout the course of a game. You can settle down your starter by telling her two or three specifics on which you want her to concentrate during that game. Instead of worrying about 100 different scenarios, she is able to focus better and stay calm.

If your desired result is to not give up any goals, you are being unrealistic, and a bad goal may throw off your game. But if your goal is to give your maximum effort for 60 minutes so your team has its best chance to win, a bad goal may easily be forgotten. If your desired result by the end of the season is to have improved your ability as much as possible in order to play at a higher level next year, you can consider a bad game as a learning tool that provides motivation to work harder.

ATTITUDE

Successful athletes maintain an attitude that allows them to have the self-confidence to perform at a high level. That attitude gives them the ability to react without hesitation. Making split-second decisions is a big part of goaltending. If you are afraid to make a mistake, you will not play to the best of your ability. Fear promotes hesitation. Hesitation creates internal second-guessing that can only lead to trouble. If you have worked hard at learning and understanding your position, this knowledge is inside of you. Your solid fundamentals will show without your having to consciously think about them. When the puck drops, let your instincts take over and have a ball!

Focus on the Positive

Everyone has a positive attitude somewhere inside of him; it is up to you to bring it forward. When you step on the ice before your next game, ask yourself this question: "How would I feel if I was not afraid?" The answer would probably be "GREAT." The chance to compete in a sport you love, playing with friends, with people cheering you on—these are the reasons you chose to play hockey in the first place. Once you've put your fears away, you can perform to the best of your abilities.

DEALING WITH A SLUMP

No one is immune to the dreaded slump, but a smart goaltender will come out of a slump faster than one who does not think about his position. Try to do the following to help you get out of a slump:

- Take advantage of your evaluations to note what kind of goals you are allowing and what you can do about them. Be determined to stop that type of shot.
- Take a new outlook or philosophy into a game and see if this new approach can give you a jump start.
- Put on a show. Go out for your next game determined to put on a big show for the fans. Exaggerate your saves a little or try a little "trash talking"—anything to provide a spark.
- Be someone else! Remember as a kid when you used to pretend you were a great NHL superstar? Why not try it again? Be Eddie Belfour or Patrick Roy: it will take the pressure off of you and place it on them!

coaches' tip

It is important to understand the motivating factors of your goaltenders. Some goaltenders are motivated to achieve success, while others are motivated by fear of failure. A player motivated to achieve success will be up for the best competition but may have trouble getting enthusiastic about playing a weak team. A player motivated by a fear of failure will look either for the easy win or for a game so tough the odds are overwhelmingly in the other team's favor.

The coach's responsibility is to identify trends in a goaltender's mental approach and improve on them. For example, if you're going into a game with a weak team and your goaltender is motivated by success, give her specific goals and challenges to inspire her play.

If your goaltender is motivated by fear of failure, work on building his confidence and creating an outlook for him that transfers responsibility to the team rather than just him.

MENTAL PREPARATION THROUGH SETTING GOALS

A big part of remaining constantly motivated during practices and games is focus. You must be clear on why you are putting in all this work and what you want to achieve. If you are unclear inside, you will not be able to perform at your highest level and will not carry the respect for yourself and for the game necessary to be a winner.

Once you initially have a clear focus, your next task is to maintain that focus, and you do that by setting goals. No one can tell you what your specific goals should be, but the following five principles will help you set goals.

1. ***Set both long and short-term goals.*** It's not enough to say, "I want to play in the NHL one day." Rather, set short-term goals such as playing Midget "AAA" or prep school, then college or major junior, and then the minors.

2. ***Make your goals realistic, but tough to achieve.*** Set a goal like finishing in the top three goaltenders in your league or winning

70 percent of your starts. The idea is to challenge yourself with a goal for which you really have to work hard.

3. ***Set goals that can be measured.*** A goal to become a better goalie is good, but you need a way to quantify your progress. Use statistics such as save percentage, number of starts, and goals against average, to make it easier for you to see the results.

4. ***Make a written plan describing how you will achieve your goals.*** Set specific criteria for improving as a goaltender. Your plan may entail more off-ice work, form and film analysis, or extra time at camps and clinics.

5. ***Evaluate, evaluate, evaluate!*** Good goal-setting requires that you continuously evaluate your progress toward achieving your goals. Make a photocopy and fill out the Goal-Setting Form provided on pages 184-185, and constantly read over it to track your results. This will provide motivation, praise, and encouragement in bringing your game to the next level.

GOAL EVALUATION FORM

One final useful tool is the Goal Evaluation Form on pages 186-187. Make several photocopies of this form and give them to a coach, parent on the bench, or your team's other goalie to fill out for you during a game. Specific notes on each goal scored against you will help provide valuable feedback, and you will be able to find areas for improvement. By studying these, you will know how to stop the puck in similar situations in the future.

PLAN FOR SUCCESS!

Goaltending is not easy. If you are mentally weak, you will have a tough time meeting the challenges and dealing with the pressure. But if you have a plan and a sound philosophy on how you will deal with the peaks and valleys inherent in the life of a goaltender, your chances of success will improve dramatically.

Goal-Setting Form

LONG-TERM GOALS

_____

_____

_____

_____

_____

_____

_____

_____

SHORT-TERM GOALS

_____

_____

_____

_____

_____

_____

_____

_____

PLAN TO ACHIEVE GOALS

_____

_____

_____

_____

_____

_____

_____

EVALUATION OF GOALS

_____

_____

_____

_____

_____

_____

_____

Goal Evaluation Form

TEAM: DATE:

SHOT

Time of goal: [   ]   Period: [   ]   Score: [   ]

Type of shot (circle one):

Slap shot

Wrist shot

Backhand

Snapshot

Deke

Where did the puck beat me?

[   ]

SHOOTER

Shooter (circle one):

Left

Right

Attack (circle one):

3-on-2

3-on-1

3-on-0

2-on-1

2-on-0

1-on-1

Breakaway

Situation (circle one):

Power play

Shorthanded

Even strength

Zone in which puck was shot?

[   ]

POSITIONING

Position (circle one):
Standing
Down
In between

Type of save attempted (circle one):
Butterfly
Half butterfly
Kick save
Glove save
Blocker save
Two pad stack
Stick save
Poke check
Half poke

Comments:
_____
_____
_____

Where was I positioned?

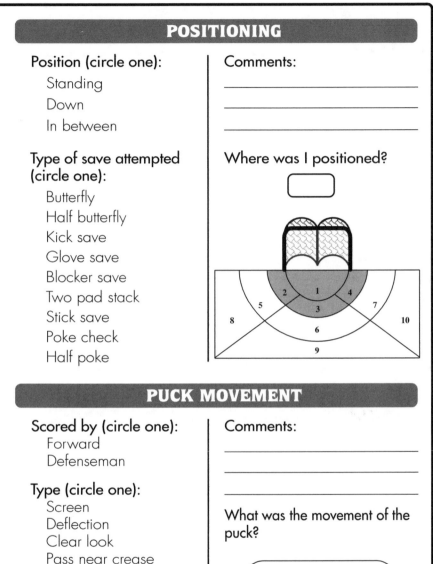

PUCK MOVEMENT

Scored by (circle one):
Forward
Defenseman

Type (circle one):
Screen
Deflection
Clear look
Pass near crease
Goalie error
Wraparound
Fluke
Rebound

Note: if goal was scored after a rebound, mark an R where rebound was left.

Comments:
_____
_____
_____

What was the movement of the puck?

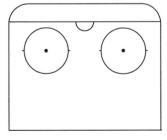

Index

About the Author

From left to right: Brent, Bill, and Tom (Huron Hockey); author Brian Daccord; Bret (Miller Goaltending Equipment)

Having played professional hockey in Europe, college hockey in the United States, and junior hockey in Canada, Brian Daccord truly brings a global perspective to the position of goaltender.

A former player and coach at Merrimack College (NCAA Division I, Hockey East), Daccord holds a masters degree in sports science and is certified by USA Hockey as a master level coach. At present, he is the head hockey coach and general manager of the Valley Junior Warriors of the Eastern Junior Hockey League and teaches goaltenders of all ages at camps and clinics throughout the year.

Daccord, a native of Montreal, lives in North Andover, Massachusetts, with his wife, Daniela, and son, Joël.

Related titles from Human Kinetics

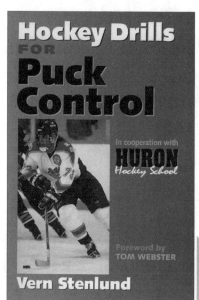

1996 • Paper • 192 pp
Item PSTE0998
ISBN 0-87322-998-3
$14.95 ($19.95 Canadian)

Control the puck and control the game. With 70 challenging drills for specific puck-control skills, your team will put more points on the scoreboard. Includes full-page diagrams and helpful ideas for refining the drills to challenge even the most experienced player.

1998 • Item MHKV0821
ISBN 0-88011-821-0
53 minute videotape
$24.95 ($36.95 Canadian)

If you're serious about becoming a top hockey player, you know every second counts on the ice. This high-action, high-instruction video presents skating workout activities performed by many NHL players. Use the tape to develop practice sessions and improve technique, speed, agility, and conditioning.

Prices subject to change.